MESHUMED!

MESHUMED!

By
ZOLA LEVITT

❧ ❧ ❧
❧ ❧ ❧

To Tom McCall,
devoted friend and able missionary to the Jews.

Library of Congress Cataloging in Publication Data

Levitt, Zola.
  Meshumed!
  CONTENTS: The atheist of Dachau: Josef Herschkowitz.
—The gestapo and the Holland saboteur: Elias den Arend.
—My son, my son! How can you be a Christian?: Elias Zim-
merman. [etc.]
  1. Converts from Judaism—Biography. I. Title.
BV2623.A1L48   248'.246   78-21111
ISBN 0-8024-5253-1

Contents

Foreword

The growth of Hebrew Christianity is an exciting phenomenon! We never dreamed it would be. When I started in Jewish missions over forty years ago, I thought I knew personally every Hebrew Christian in the United States and Canada. It seemed that we were so few.

Things have changed, and there are now large numbers of Hebrew Christians all over the world. They come from all walks of life—the old, the young, professionals, artists, teachers. They are radiant, articulate, and talented. Not only are many of them missionaries to their own people, but also many are leaders in the modern worldwide mission of the church of Christ.

We should not be surprised at this phenomenon. Hebrew Christians have been prominent in all of the great expansional thrusts of the church. They sparked the worldwide witness of the first century. An anonymous writer researched this subject and wrote an article called "The Dedicated Dozen."

> These men covered more ground than the armies of Caesar, Alexander, or Cyrus. . . .
>
> Paul and Thomas probably traveled further than the other apostles. Paul made four famous missionary journeys, ending in Spain. Nero took Paul's life at Rome in 67 A.D.
>
> Thomas preached in Persia and then in India. He was slain near Madras.
>
> James the Greater was the first martyred apostle. He died at the hand of Herod in 44 A.D.

Nathanael (Bartholomew) may have also reached India. He was flayed alive by King Astyages of Armenia.

Matthew went as far as Ethiopia and was slain in Persia.

Peter, at his request, was crucified head downward by Nero.

Andrew ministered in Greece and was crucified at Achaia.

John superintended the churches in Asia. He was plunged into a boiling cauldron but was miraculously saved. He was the only apostle to die a natural death.

Philip preached in Phrygia (Turkey) and died by crucifixion.

James the Less was the first bishop at Jerusalem. He was thrown from a tower, stoned, and clubbed to death in 62 A.D.

Jude preached in Arabia, Persia, Mesopotamia, and Syria, where he suffered martyrdom.

Simon preached in Egypt and was slain at Suanir.

Matthias moved through Asia Minor. He was put to death at Colchis on the Black Sea.

Barnabas was martyred at Cyprus during Nero's reign. They took it this far . . . How far will YOU take it?*

These were all Hebrew Christians. It was a Hebrew Christian, Nicolaus de Lyra, who inspired Martin Luther's literal interpretation of Scripture and made the Reformation possible. There is a Latin saying: *Si Lyra non lyrasset, Lutherus non saltasset*—"If Lyra had not played on his lyre, Luther could not have danced."

Hebrew Christians were also very prominent in the nineteenth- and early-twentieth-century revival of missions. Among the best known were Isadore Loewenthal, the trailblazer to Afghanistan; Solomon Ginsburg, pioneer in Brazil; and Bishop Samuel Isaac Joseph Schereschewsky,

*"The Dedicated Dozen," *The Chosen People*, January 1958, pp. 3-4.

whose translations of the Scriptures into Mandarin and Easy Wenli dialects of China are still classics.

This book will help bring you up-to-date in the field of Jewish evangelism. It presents just a small sampling of the many in Israel who "have found him, of whom Moses in the law, and the prophets, did write, Jesus of Nazareth" (John 1:45). We thank God for these modern stalwarts of the faith. There are many thousands more.

DANIEL FUCHS

1

The Atheist of Dachau

JOSEF HERSCHKOWITZ

Josef just didn't understand.

To see men hate each other—that he could understand. To see men hate particularly the Jews—that was understandable. In fact it was practically a tradition. To see military men intern certain peoples in concentration camps— well, that had happened before; that he could understand, too.

But here at Dachau Concentration Camp in 1938, his understanding of things was being put to a new test. Cruelty for its own sake was simply entirely new to him.

How was he to understand one man strapping down another in the sunlight and burning out his eyes with a magnifying glass? What did it really mean when men chose to burn a fellowman to death, inch by inch, with cigarette butts? How was he to fathom the reasons behind activities such as the insertion of a compressed-air hose into the anus of a human being for the purpose of inflating his torso until it blew up like a grotesque balloon? Why did men drown other men with water hoses?

JOSEF HERSCHKOWITZ (October 15, 1898-March 25, 1971) founded the Minneapolis branch of the American Board of Missions to the Jews.

Josef was an atheist. He didn't know a lot about "evil." He didn't believe in a devil, and he certainly didn't believe in God.

He simply was not spiritually equipped to appreciate the level of evil he was seeing. He was perplexed.

On the past Yom Kippur—the Day of Atonement—Hitler had ordered all the synagogues burned. Josef was arrested, along with five thousand other Jewish men, because the arson was inexplicably blamed on the Jews. He had stood at attention for five days and four nights without food or water, without rest, without the slightest pause. He dared not fall, as some of the weakened men did, because the SS (*Schutzstaffel*) officer in charge would have stomped his face and body with his heavy jackboots.

After that ordeal, the survivors were packed into boxcars, hundreds to a car, in standing positions, and they traveled through the night to Dachau, near Munich. At the concentration camp, Josef lost track of his companions from Vienna as Jews were crowded into small rooms for some sort of cataloging by their captors.

In Josef's room, sleep was impossible. People stood shoulder to shoulder, and they had to organize ways to lie on each other for equal periods in order to rest. The door would open occasionally for "meals" consisting of a little tapioca, barley, or processed whale meat.

Josef's atheism was not adequate for the occasion. It gave him nowhere to turn, since he had no God and therefore no higher authority to whom to appeal for help. And it gave him no comprehension of what was happening around him. Atheism does not believe in some ultimate "good," so it is very limited in considering some ultimate "bad." Things were just far too bad for Josef's meager understanding of spiritual matters.

And his atheism had a very ironic quality now that he was being so severely punished for being of the wrong religious persuasion. Josef's last name was Herschkowitz, a name fit only for a tombstone—if that—under the new regime.

It was not only Jews, however, who were being persecuted at Dachau. Josef observed a contingent of Christians—German Protestant pastors—that was placed in a special barbed-wire-enclosed compound. These unfortunates were called upon to renounce their allegiance to Jesus Christ, in keeping with the new regime. Josef's atheism grew ugly in his own mind as he realized that his only philosophical compatriots in the camp were the Nazis themselves.

The pastors impressed Josef very much because they were strong and stubborn. They did not *have* to suffer, as the Jews did; they needed only to sign an affidavit stating that Hitler, not Christ, was their leader, and they would be immediately released. They had carte blanche to leave Dachau. But they were peculiar men indeed; they refused.

Josef watched them, a thousand strong, at their prayers. The SS officer would come by with his affidavit and pick out a prisoner at random. "Who is your leader?" he would ask simply. "Christ," the churchman would answer.

The officer would club the man to the ground and begin to kick at his head until he rose. Then he would ask him again, "Who is your leader?"

The reply would be the same, and the punishment would be reenacted. Josef, profoundly moved, watched one day as the same pastor underwent the same treatment for more than half an hour. Toward the end, before the pastor died from the steady battering, the muffled name "Christi" could barely be understood. The man's jaw was broken,

and his teeth protruded through his lips. But he was able
to pronounce the name of his Lord until the very end. Only
when the Christian's skull was utterly shattered did the
name of the Savior cease to come from his mouth.

The scene took Josef back.

He had a bleak present and certainly no future, so his
mind went back into his life in search of the source of those
pastors' strength. Religion was a thing he had lived without since his youth, and he was perplexed.

Josef was born in Vienna about the turn of the century,
and his parents were strict Orthodox Jews. He was carefully reared in all of the traditions and concepts of Judaism—particularly in its unflinching opposition to what it
considered to be Christianity. Josef was taught that there
were two kinds of people in the world—Jews and Christians.

As a youth he was often beaten black and blue by those
termed "Christians." They shouted, "Christ killer!" at him,
and he became understandably opposed to this madness
known as Christianity. Had he subscribed to any New
Testament Scripture in those days, it would have been
John 1:46—"Can there any good thing come out of Nazareth?"

He wasn't satisfied with Judaism either as he grew up,
and at seventeen, when the First World War broke out,
he was entirely "fed up" with religion. He gave his stricken
father his prayer book and announced, "I don't believe in
an almighty God."

He fell in love with a Gentile girl who also was an atheist,
and at pain of each of them being disowned for the liaison,
he married her. They had to "go it alone," without families
or God, without synagogue or church.

They loved each other, however, and they lived out fifteen years of happily married life, until March 12, 1938. That was the day Hitler's troops goose-stepped into Austria.

Josef had a good position as an engineer, and Hermina, his wife, was the supervising nurse in Vienna's largest mental hospital. But from the moment of the entrance of the Nazis, Josef and Hermina's lives were turned upside down.

Jewish persecution began on a scale incomprehensible to anyone who was not there at the time. No Jew could keep a job. Grocery stores displayed signs: "No gypsies, no dogs, no Jews." Jewish women were dragged from their homes and made to scrub the streets and the staff cars of the SS officers—in the more reportable encounters. The black-shirted Nazis broke into Jewish homes on any pretense, robbing and raping. If a husband tried to defend his wife, he was shot. If children cried, they were disposed of out the windows—through the glass and down to the street, even from upper floors.

The Jews, totally panicky, lined up in Vienna at the consulates of various nations, begging for admission to any other country. But the question always came, "Are you a Jew?" An affirmative answer brought flat refusal, unless the applicant were very well-to-do. Few of these unemployed unfortunates were in a position to bribe their way to freedom.

In effect, the whole world was closed to the Jews, and they were completely trapped with those who hated them. There simply was no help available.

That was when Hermina suggested the Christian mission downtown. "They help Jews," was all she said, and it was enough. Josef at once went to the mission. He didn't quite know what to expect, but this was a life-and-death matter, and he was flexible, in an atheistic sort of way.

Josef found a Christian Jew at the mission, and he considered him a traitor. What little respect he still had for Judaism, and what little memory he had of his upbringing and his training, still included hatred of the "Christians," and a special detesting of the "vermin" who converted to the side of the enemy.

He began by saying, "Reverend, I'm a Jew and an atheist. My wife sent me here. But I'm not going to sell my soul for anything!"

The pastor looked him over. "Did I ask you to sell anything?" he asked.

Josef was embarrassed. "Look," he said, "my wife said I could get help here."

"You can, in the name of Jesus Christ."

The name fell on his ears like a sledgehammer blow. But he had no choice. The mission took him in and protected him.

He had to listen to the gospel, of course, as told by his original interviewer, the Reverend Emanuel Lichtenstein, the son of a Hungarian rabbi. He despised the gospel. He was quoted as saying he was glad he had two ears—one where the gospel could go in and one where it could go out.

Safe within the shelter of the mission, Josef could often hear the cries of those tortured to death in the streets outside. Then came the fateful Day of Atonement, and a true day of reckoning it was. And now Josef suffered at Dachau, still unable to understand.

The mission had been helpless to protect Josef and the other Jews once the Nazis got down to their real business in Austria—finding and killing every last Jew, slowly. But at least those who were taken from the mission, even the unsaved, had some portion of the gospel to contemplate. Josef had sat through a number of teaching sessions with Emanuel Lichtenstein, and what a man has in his heart goes with him everywhere.

Now, at Dachau, where his very life hung by a thread, Josef struggled to understand godly things. Life and death were godly things, or at least very important things about which any man thinks "spiritually." Even an atheist respects death. Josef thought hard.

He had at least three sources of instruction about God available to him: he had his childhood teachings about the Father in heaven; he had his instruction at the Hebrew Christian mission in Vienna; and he noticed one day that the shiny belt buckle of each SS officer bore the engraved legend *Gott Mit Uns* (God is with us).

That last message had Josef really wondering about God. Even as an atheist, Josef wasn't ready to relegate God to the SS.

From somewhere in Josef's brain came odd memories of Scripture he had been taught—maybe when a boy, maybe when in the mission. As he watched the multitudes murdered all around him, his mind repeated, "A thousand shall fall at thy side, and ten thousand at thy right hand; but it shall not come nigh thee."* It was a hopeful thought. Josef wasn't certain he had the words right, but it somehow gave him a sense of having a "guardian angel"—that someone, somewhere, cared about whether an unfortunate named Herschkowitz survived.

One day a fellow standing immediately beside Josef was beaten to death. Josef stood quivering, covered with blood, and he found himself saying in his heart, "Thank You,

*Psalm 91:7.

God." Surely, it was only the reasonable thought of a person who had just barely escaped death; but then again, if there was an angel on guard, could there just as well be a God?

Josef stopped fooling himself. Perhaps his atheism had endured twenty years, but the matter was now clear in his heart. He had come to believe in God.

It was a great relief.

The Nazis slaughtered seventeen thousand Jewish people at Dachau, but Josef Herschkowitz was not to be one of them. While he suffered the horror of the concentration camp, his faithful wife was working furiously for his release. The Nazis could be approached by a Gentile, like Hermina, and if she could make a case for her husband's release, it might be possible. The Nazis were only interested in getting rid of Jews; where they went was of little concern, if they just went away. Far. If Hermina could save them the trouble of one extra execution, and if they could be assured that they would never see this particular "subhuman" (their term) again, they might let him go.

Hermina bought Josef a railroad ticket to Shanghai, China. She then contacted a sympathetic former fellow employee of Josef's in the Vienna city hall to enlist his help in pleading with the Gestapo, the Nazi police.

She approached the Gestapo with the ticket and the friend and begged for her husband's life.

It took six months of begging, but at last the Nazis relented. Josef became one of the paltry few who slipped through their fingers in that early part of the persecution.

When Josef, not believing his good fortune, arrived back in Vienna, he immediately contacted Emanuel Lichtenstein, who, for all his religious "faults," was a trustworthy friend. The pastor advised strongly against Shanghai. War was raging there; employment would be impossible. Praise God that Josef was free, but Shanghai was not the place for him.

Emanuel Lichtenstein had a better idea. His mission had good connections. It was, he revealed, a branch of the American Board of Missions to the Jews (ABMJ). The mission itself could arrange to send Josef to Holland. Things were much better there.

Other men needed to be spirited out of Vienna to the Protestant refugee shelter at Camp Sluis, Holland, however, and Hermina declined to go with Josef, not wanting to take up precious space. She herself was in no danger from the Nazis as yet. She assumed that she could join her husband shorlty thereafter. But it did not work out that way.

She was not to see him for many years.

One hundred fifty families were housed at the shelter when Josef arrived. Almost all of them were Hebrew Christians, and all were studying the New Testament. Pastor Benfry, the German Lutheran clergyman of the camp, interviewed the new arrival briefly. Josef told him, "I've lost my ability to read Hebrew, but I'd like to learn how to pray."

And he made very clear: "Of course, I don't believe in Christ."

"Do you really believe in God?" the pastor asked.

Josef said that he did, and the pastor concluded, "Then we will leave it up to Him. The Holy Spirit will reveal to you what you ought to do."

Josef did not quibble about the Holy Spirit (whatever *that* was) but accepted his new sanctuary and its attendant New Testament study. For ten months he studied the gospel while he frantically wrote letters to any address anywhere in the world where someone might sign an affidavit of support so that he could emigrate. Back in Vienna, Hermina was doing the same thing. If they only could uncover—anywhere—a sponsor, they could leave the increasingly dangerous European scene.

One day Pastor Benfry delicately approached again the question of Josef's beliefs. After all, the man had been studying the New Testament for almost a year; had he thought about coming to the Messiah? Did he want to be baptized now?

Josef answered, "No. I am a Jew."

Only days later, Hermina sent Josef an affidavit signed by a Blair family in the United States. The Blairs were willing to sponsor one Jew, and Hermina had faithfully referred the precious document to her husband.

There were many problems still. The Blairs did not show a suitable income to sponsor an immigrant. The American consul in Holland would have to rule on the weak affidavit, and that would take time. The Germans were about to march on Holland. If Josef did get an affirmative judgment on the visa in time, any boat trip out of Holland would be terribly hazardous; the Germans would freely torpedo any ship they spotted in Dutch waters.

It was a time for prayer, even for marginal believers. Josef uttered a unique request, addressed to the Father in heaven: "If Jesus is the Messiah, move the heart of the consul to grant the visa."

The visa was granted. Josef boarded the *last* boat for America. The ship got through. The new immigrant arrived in New York City on May 16, 1940.

He tried, without success to find work in New York, but reported to the Blair home in Erie, Pennsylvania after two weeks in the New World. He spoke not a word of English and had no form of livelihood.

But he knew that he was safe and that his prayer concerning Jesus Christ had been fully answered. He accompanied the Blairs to their little Baptist church and listened to their testimony. He was saved and baptized there.

Hermina knew none of this. Attempts to get her to the United States grew more hopeless as the Nazis took over Europe, until finally correspondence with Austria was stopped. The American consul left Germany, and there was no further hope of Hermina's emigration. There was but one letter from her during the war years, through the Red Cross, and it was a tonic to Josef. It arrived as he was recovering from a severe heart attack, and he felt the hand of God at the crucial moment again.

At the end of 1945 Josef finally received a lengthy letter from Hermina. He learned that the Nazis had pressured her to divorce her husband and had taken away her hospital position when she refused. She lived on a meager pension in Vienna, helping the Jews amid all the atrocities.

In early 1946 she sent a snapshot, and it made Josef weep. She looked starved; she had lost half her weight. He shipped her foodstuffs and frantically renewed his efforts to get her to the United States. Josef himself became an American citizen. Fervently he continued in prayer for his wife as the Russians entered Vienna.

And Josef's prayers were answered again. Vienna was partitioned, and Hermina found herself in the American zone. Seemingly God had moved in world politics to place one servant's wife in a territory occupied by his new homeland. It became a much simpler matter to restore the wife of an American citizen than it had been to emigrate the Gentile wife of a homeless Jew from a Nazi province. In early 1947, Hermina boarded a ship for America and the husband she had not seen for some eight years.

Josef was a different person now. In his American life he had gone to Bible school (New Testament!), done many kinds of work (including feeding hogs), and had gained quite a bit of weight. He was almost bald, was weakened by his heart condition, now wore glasses for the first time, and was a preacher of the gospel! Would Hermina even recognize this man she had formerly lived with for fifteen years?

It was a dramatic encounter. Josef came to meet her ship and had to wait three agonizing days, as it was delayed in crossing. Hermina used the time to work on her wan appearance. She ate well and stayed in the sun. Few on the dock could appreciate the tension of that first moment when she debarked.

Josef would not have quibbled about the appearance of his faithful wife, who had purchased his release from Dachau, who had endured the war years under the Nazis and the occupation under the Soviets, who had passed up every opportunity for her own escape in favor of the survival of her husband. He loved her, and he ached for her.

They were nervous strangers at first, afraid to smile, afraid to speak. What could be expected after all? Josef opened Hermina's suitcase and tossed out a rotten orange. She wept. A rotten orange was good food in the Vienna she had just left. Josef determined to feed his wife and to restore her emaciated body. He purposely took her on a tour of food stores to show her that her days of hunger, of rotten foods, were over. He showed her refrigerators, washing machines, the abundance of automobiles and appliances of all sorts.

Hermina was in a dream world. Most fascinating of all to her were the powerful receiving sets of the American radio industry. How many years had she hidden under three pillows her tiny, static-prone radio so that the Gestapo would not detect her listening to the world news!

There was one serious matter to be taken care of at once. They were now no longer atheist and atheist. They were now Christian and Gentile. Carefully, tenderly, Josef Herschkowitz testified to his wife of Jesus Christ.

In eight days Hermina was able to apprehend the difference in her husband, and she could see that his Christian testimony was sincere and powerful. Josef's ministry at that time was with the American Board of Missions to the Jews, the very organization he had resorted to in desperation back in Vienna. He was at that point a field worker, filling speaking engagements and exhorting the Jewish people to come to their Messiah. He worked with Gentile Christians to persuade them to extend their witness to their Jewish neighbors. His testimony was obviously powerful and effective. He could say that God literally had given him life and that the Messiah had given His promised abundance.

The faithful Hermina joined Josef in worship of Christ, coming to the Savior on the eighth day after her arrival, and she dedicated herself to something at which she was already somewhat expert.

She became a helpmeet to her husband.

2

The Gestapo and the Holland Saboteur

ELIAS DEN AREND

The career of the atheist of Dachau might have seemed luxury-filled to Elias den Arend. Josef Herschkowitz had been interned and released, after all. Dr. Arend and his family were hunted down like animals for seven years.

He had asked for it. He was a member of the Jewish underground in Holland. He defied the Nazi overlords and challenged the Gestapo for the lives of his countrymen day after day. He carried false papers, ate out of garbage cans, and lived the terrifying life of a partisan zealot, standing stubbornly between the atrocities of the Third Reich and the Jewish people.

He really wasn't cut out for it. Gentle, scholarly Elias den Arend held a teacher's certificate from a Dutch university and the doctorate in music, for which he studied in Leipzig, Germany. He had been born and brought up in the Netherlands in a fairly well-to-do merchant family, and he was in no way prepared for the life of a freedom fighter.

At the outbreak of hostilities in 1939, Elias lived with his wife and son in Breda, Netherlands, a land invaded and oc-

---

ELIAS DEN AREND (August 25, 1907–) is a field evangelist for the American Board of Missions to the Jews.

cupied immediately by the Nazis. The ruthless transfers
of the Jewish citizens to concentration camps began at
once, but Elias was spared. He was thought of as being
useful to the Reich, which in some sectors had set up separate schooling for Jewish children. Politically, it served
the Nazi theory of the inferiority of Jews to drive their
children out of the public schools. Jewish teachers had to
be selected for them, to carry on the implication that teachers of the Reich could not be bothered with instructing
subhumans.

They made a slight mistake in choosing Dr. Arend. They
may have assumed that the learned, German-educated musician would be too preoccupied with the things of philoso-
phy to care to resist the oppression going on around him,
but they were wrong. The professor cheated them out of
many Jewish lives.

The newly appointed teacher had difficulty in keeping
his roll book. Children kept disappearing. One by one
they were gone as the Nazis raided Jewish homes at night
and spirited away even little children to the camps. Elias
realized that those children would never be seen again, and
he became angry. Soon he joined the resistance movement
and took training as a saboteur.

Jewish saboteurs did not have the privilege of really
fighting back. The odds were entirely hopeless, and the
willingness of the enemy to murder women and children
made them turn their attention to hiding places. The important thing was to protect Jewish lives, especially the de-
fenseless. True armed resistance was virtually out of the
question.

In school, where Elias maintained his position, the children asked him to pray for them. The logic escaped him,

however. If there was an all-powerful God, why was it even necessary to ask Him to save these innocent ones? No, he could not pray to a God who had obviously abandoned needy human souls. He felt almost superior to a God of such indifference.

Mrs. Arend did not feel that way at all. This was definitely a time for prayer, she felt, and she prayed daily with her son, particularly asking God for the Messiah. The mighty Messiah of Israel, she believed, could stem the tide and deliver the chosen people from this massacre. The Redeemer could cast away the Nazis.

Elias's wife was to pray for the Messiah to come so often and so intensely that He did come to her one day. She eventually came somehow to the knowledge that Jesus Christ was the promised One of Israel, and she trusted completely in Him for her salvation. Elias almost ridiculed her for this obtuse conclusion; God Himself was useless enough in their circumstances, but how could she ask the Gentile God for help? Elias felt true contempt for those who prayed while the Nazis steadily reduced their number.

Elias did have to grant that the Christian families, those "born again" types, could be counted on to hide the Jews. Their homes were open, despite the dangers involved, and Elias learned to discriminate, out of necessity, true Christians from those who were merely Gentiles. The work was demanding and utterly secret—even Elias's wife and son did not know that he was with the underground or dependent on the Christians.

The day finally came when a hiding place became necessary for Elias himself. The Nazis had caught on; the mild-mannered teacher was behind a lot of the hiding of Jews that was going on. If they found him, they would kill him on the spot; he would not have to be troubled about a concentration camp.

Elias and his family fled, entirely too "hot" for anyone to try to hide locally. Traveling with false credentials and passing checkpoints with their hearts in their mouths, they went to the southern part of the Netherlands to the home of a fellow underground worker. But when they arrived at their sanctuary, they found that the place was under surveillance—the man of the house himself had already fled.

Unable to go any farther, they decided to stay just one night, with the permission of the trembling family of the compatriot. They were exhausted.

Elias would have valued a full night's rest, but he was awakened by his panicky wife at 4:00 or 5:00 in the morning. She had been talking to God, she said, and He had told her, "Get out of this house quickly; danger is near!"

The weary saboteur could only laugh at her. Why would God decide to speak up *now?* For all His uncaring attitude toward His chosen people, couldn't He let one family at least rest for one night? What sort of unwelcome miracle was this ridiculous effort of God? It struck him as practically funny. If God had, at His leisure, finally opted to protect them—well, He had missed plenty of good chances previously. "Let me rest," Elias told his stricken wife.

But Mrs. Arend prevailed. Her tears, her horrible fear, and her complete conviction that she had indeed heard the very voice of God finally convinced Elias. He arose and took his family out of the house just before dawn.

The Gestapo arrived minutes later, and found nothing.

They journeyed on, finally finding a relatively quiet situation with the underground in another city. Here Elias's wife and son could be secreted in a hiding place, and he could visit with them now and then. Elias himself kept moving and continued his work against the Nazis. His wife was now aware of, and proud of, what he was really doing, and her prayers changed character. Now she prayed constantly that the Lord would walk with her courageous husband and defend him against his powerful enemies. She seemed confident that Elias would be watched over.

For his part, the saboteur, becoming accustomed to and almost cynical about his constant danger, still thought his wife was very foolish. She was praying about matters she had little knowledge of, for one thing. The men of the underground did not give their wives details of their work; there was a good chance that the information could be gotten out of these women with whips and rapings some future day. Elias went about his grim work closemouthed, while his wife entreated God on his behalf.

They were able to survive by means of false ration cards provided by an underground man who worked in the Nazi administration. All food was rationed, or had to be purchased at exorbitant prices through the black market that was operating throughout the country. The ration cards had to be constantly renewed by the ordinary citizens, but the underground workers received theirs directly from the planted saboteur.

Then he was caught.

It was shattering news for Elias and his family. This meant literally the end of their food supply. There was no other way to obtain the precious cards; the risk was too great.

Elias began to purchase his food on the black market and was quickly "picked clean." In a few weeks the Arends had neither food nor money.

Elias counseled his wife that they should commit suicide.

Many Jews were taking this way out, he said, and it now
made good sense. He could be of no further use to the underground. They could die with some dignity, rather than
being executed like criminals by the Nazis, and they could
finish their lives together, right there in the hiding place.
Elias planned to kill his wife and son and then take his own
life.

What alternative did they have, after all? If they came
out of their hiding place the Nazis would pounce. Elias
was on their "most wanted" list—perhaps right at the top
of it. He would greatly suffer for his courage. And when
the Nazis finished with Elias, they would begin on his wife,
and even the child. They had shown no squeamishness
over torturing women and children if there was a chance
of getting some information, or even just for the pleasure
of it. No, this must never happen, Elias told his wife. They
must die now, while they had a chance to choose their way
of death.

Mrs. Arend didn't know how to argue with this conclusion. Her husband was right, she now thought. If they
couldn't eat, then sooner or later they had to come out of
hiding. And that was simply unthinkable.

But she still believed God would help them. She told
Elias that she would pray, and this time he didn't even
bother to laugh at her. In deference to his total frustration,
she asked for only one day. She would go to God for help,
and if He didn't respond in one day, she would follow her
husband in suicide. Elias granted the request, more out
of wanting to put off the moment of killing his loved ones
than out of any faith in God.

He went to sleep very hungry on what he believed to be
his last earthly night. His wife stayed awake, talking with
God.

She was radiant the following morning. Even Elias was impressed. Nothing had happened—no guardian angel had come out of the night—but Mrs. Arend was calm and totally convinced that their troubles were over.

Later in the morning, she was hardly surprised to find an envelope with cash in it on the floor outside their door. A note with the money said simply, "More follows. A friend." They afterwards found out that the money had been provided by the wife of the incarcerated ration card man. She had taken up her husband's work, finding his contacts and providing them with what she could.

With embarrassment about his own lack of faith, Elias watched his wife and son thank God. But there was further work to be done and further precautions to be taken. The saboteur was not quite ready just to rest in the Lord.

They had more grief and more trials, needless to say. The situation grew steadily more intense. Their Jewish faces became more obvious in the absence of so many others. They stuck out like sore thumbs.

When it was necessary to travel to another hiding place by train, Elias's wife committed the travel to the Lord, and they rode undetected in a train coach filled with Nazis. They arrived at their new hiding place without further trouble. Elias heard his wife whisper to the Lord, "How great Thou art!"

From hiding place to hiding place the Arends went, passing the entire war in seclusion and dread. Elias went on with his underground work, and his wife and son went on with their hiding. Late in the war the furious Nazis, bedeviled by their constant defeats, went after the Jews with renewed vigor. The Arends were hiding in a Christian household that was raided by the Gestapo five times in one day, but they were still undiscovered!

By this time Elias had begun to make his peace with God. He began to understand that he had not escaped detection so many times purely by accident. He was some kind of special case, he realized. His rational professor's mind could not accept that he had merely been lucky. So many had perished, but the Arends had not, in fact, been deserted by God, as Elias had once thought.

"I had deserted *Him*," Elias admitted finally, "because I had so little faith that He was a God who answered prayer. But now things were different, and I yielded myself to Him as my Savior, Redeemer, and Messiah." Elias came to Jesus Christ, and he and his family were now three Christians.

Elias could remember his father's admonition many years before: "Wait, my son, until the Messiah comes." Well, the Messiah had now come for Elias, and he was more than ready.

There were more dangers, but the Arends, veterans of enduring terror and united as Christians, survived until 1945, when the war at last ended. When the final battle had been fought, and the Nazis had been routed out of Holland entirely, it was time to regroup the family and take a count.

But there was no one left to count. They had all been murdered by the Nazis—every relative on Elias's side and everyone on his wife's side. They alone of their family had survived the holocaust.

That settled matters in Europe for Elias. He determined to take his family to America and to start a new life, far from the ugly memories, the hiding places, and the empty homes of the Jewish community.

They landed in New York in the summer of 1947, and Elias, musician and freedom fighter, set about looking for work. He got out of a subway at the wrong stop one day, at Seventy-second Street on the west side of Manhattan, and chanced to walk by the former headquarters building of the American Board of Missions to the Jews.

A Jewish Christian, he was immediately interested in the window display of the mission. He was particularly fascinated by a poem on display:

THE JEW

Scattered by God's almighty hand,
   Afflicted and forlorn,
Sad wanderers from their pleasant Land,
   Do Judah's children mourn;
And e'en in Christian counties, few
Breathe thoughts of pity for the Jew.

Yet listen, Gentile, do you love
   The Bible's precious page?
Then let your heart with kindness move
   To Israel's heritage;
Who traced those lines of love for you?
Each sacred writer was a Jew.

And then as years and ages passed,
   And Nations rose and fell,
Though clouds and darkness oft were cast
   O'er captive Israel
The oracles of God for you
Were kept in safety by the Jew.

And when the great Redeemer came
   For guilty man to bleed.
He did not take an angel's name,
   No, born of Abraham's seed,
Jesus, who gave His life for you—
The gentle Saviour—was a Jew.

And though His own received Him not,
    And turned in pride away,
Whence is the Gentile's happier lot?
    Are you more just than they?
No! God in pity turned to you—
Have you no pity for the Jew?

Go, then, and bend your knee to pray
    For Israel's ancient race;
Ask the dear Saviour every day
    To call them by His grace.
Go, for a debt of love is due
From Christian Gentiles to the Jew.

                              —Author Unknown

Elias entered the mission and approached the information desk. This was something entirely new to him.

Dr. Joseph Cohn, general secretary of the mission, happened by and was glad to receive the immigrant in his office. Dr. Daniel Fuchs joined the two for the telling of the
testimony of Elias Arend, a story to overwhelm even those
seasoned caretakers of troubled Jews. They were, of course,
delighted to hear of Elias's belief in the Messiah, and they
could see the possibilities of putting him to work for the
mission.

Elias was able to submit some credentials from Holland,
and while verification procedures went on across the Atlantic, he gladly accepted the job of elevator operator in
the mission headquarters. During the next two months
Elias operated his elevator, always in prayer, asking the
Lord if this were His will. Should he end up as a missionary to the Jews? Was this possibly the task for which God
had spared him? He could certainly recommend the Messiah!

Finally Elias joined the staff as a missionary. He began serious studies and was ordained in the Christian ministry in 1949. He started with the ABMJ as an itinerant field evangelist.

Today he serves as field evangelist for California and the neighboring states, testifying of his faith. He can surely verify that "Jesus saves."

Elias is fond of quoting a Scripture from Psalm 55 that had proved a great comfort to him in Holland during the war: "Give ear to my prayer, O God; and hide not thyself from my supplication. . . . Because of the voice of the enemy, because of the oppression of the wicked: for they cast iniquity upon me, and in wrath they hate me. . . . As for me, I will call upon God; and the LORD shall save me."

3

"My Son, My Son! How Can You Be a Christian?"

ELIAS ZIMMERMAN

The ministry of Elias Zimmerman spanned almost the entire globe. He traveled not between churches, as some do, nor between nations; God called "Zimmie" to cross continents and oceans in his ministry to his people.

He was obliged to virtually flee his own family on three continents and to become an orphan for Christ. He raised himself, in effect, educated himself, and always answered the call of the Lord.

Zimmie came by the name *Elias* very honestly. He was born Passover night, 1892. Since there is a moment in the Passover feast when the Jews await the coming of the prophet Elias (Elijah) to announce the Messiah, and since the baby boy came along instead, the family called him Elias.

They never dreamed that this Elias would indeed spend his lifetime announcing to the Jews that the Messiah had in fact come!

ELIAS ZIMMERMAN (April 14, 1892–) is the founder of the Los Angeles branch of the American Board of Missions to the Jews.

Zimmie's upbringing was Orthodox to the extreme; his father was an Orthodox rabbi, deeply prayerful, and committed to keeping the Law. Zimmie's first words were prayers, particularly the Sh'ma: "Hear, O Israel, the Lord our God, the Lord is one." The little child repeated this singular formula three times each day in keeping with the rite prescribed by law. Zimmie was a first-class Orthodox Jew almost before he was weaned.

At the age of five, Zimmie began his formal studies of Judaism, the Hebrew language, the Old Testament, and the Jewish laws and customs. He was enrolled in Cheder— Hebrew school—along with the other Jewish children of his town, and he was being groomed to follow in his father's footsteps. He wore the long, curled sideburns of the Orthodox tradition, and he walked about the streets looking like a miniature Talmudic scholar.

All this happened in Czarist Russia, a place where Judaism was not the most comfortable of life-styles, but where it was kept strictly, in all its glory. The Jews had had many troubles with the local Gentiles, particularly with the officialdom of the Eastern Orthodox Church, who at one time systematically sealed off Jewish neighborhoods in an attempt at conversion by starvation. Zimmie had heard the stories of churchmen leading their congregations against the chosen people in bizarre demonstrations of obedience to their detested Savior, but the stories only made him more determined in his Judaism. That was very typical of the Russian Jews.

Zimmie's upbringing, then, was very much like that shown in *Fiddler on the Roof*, the time and place being quite similar. And Zimmie, like Tevye, the hero of *Fiddler,* might well have told God, "I know we're Your chosen people, but why don't You choose somebody else for a while!"

Zimmie's father planned quite a bar mitzvah when the youngster came of age, and the leading Jews of the community all gathered at the great banquet. The thirteen-year-old Elias was now a son of the covenant with Abraham and Moses, a full-fledged Jew responsible for his behavior before God. He was presented with philacteries, little boxes containing Scripture, which he would now don during his morning prayers, except on Sabbath and the holy days. Zimmie was instructed soberly in how to be a Jew, and he had the honor of reading the Scripture portion that memorable morning.

Before Zimmie had fully recovered from officially becoming a man, his father sent him off to rabbinical school. The thirteen-year-old scholar left home to attend to serious study toward becoming a rabbi like his father. He was to train at the famed Vilner Jeshiva, one of the most celebrated and difficult rabbinical training academies in the world.

There, in Vilna, Russia, Zimmie first encountered the Messiah. He was by this time, at eighteen years of age, a talented, knowledgeable scholar of Judaism, expert in the laws and traditions of his people, and learned in the Scriptures. But he stumbled upon a simple tract discarded in a public street.

Sometimes Christians underestimate the power of a tract. Sometimes they think tracts are a waste of paper, obvious and unconvincing, self-congratulatory and banal. But the open-minded Zimmie, for all his knowledge of Judaism and all his caution toward the "enemy," was intrigued by what he read.

The tract had apparently been handed out by a missionary to the Jews, and it had ended up forsaken on the pavement. Its message was simple, but inflammatory to Jews;

Jesus Christ was the Messiah, it said, and He was crucified to save His people.

Anyone who knew Zimmie would have said that such a pamphlet had no chance with the adept young scholar. Perhaps a more subtle approach—a discussion of prophecy from the Old Testament, or a search of the practices of sacrifice for remission of sins—might have impressed the dedicated Zimmie. But a simple proclamation of the gospel? What chance did that have?

Actually, Zimmie's open heart was very convicted. He was impressed by Jesus, the human sacrifice. It was the very first time he had read anything about Jesus Christ, and he found a strange longing in his heart to know more.

The missionary's address was on the tract. Zimmie decided to contact the man.

He went by night, like Nicodemus, and he was greeted by several Jewish Christians. They welcomed him with open arms and interrupted each other in telling Zimmie exuberantly how they each had come to know the Messiah. They explained the gospel and its logical fulfillment of the Old Testament. They astounded their visitor, who was well aware of prophecy and the implications of the Jewish Scriptures about the Messiah. Zimmie recoiled from their statement that he, an accomplished rabbinical student, must accept Christ.

The missionaries pressed Zimmie to accept a copy of the New Testament and study it. The devoted youth had never shied away from books, but this was something different, of course. At length he accepted their gift and went on his way, hiding the contraband book under his coat.

In his heart he thought, *I must find out.*

Experienced reader of Scripture that he was, Zimmie gobbled up the New Testament quickly. And as he read, he saw truth. He compared the gospel very carefully with the Old Testament prophecies and types, placing the strange Scriptures under the harsh light of thorough, scholarly examination. He tried to fault the verses he read about the Messiah; he tried to invalidate the remarkable statements of Christ. He fought with the inevitable truth that slowly advanced upon him as he studied. He intensively examined Moses and the prophets, comparing word with word, prophecy with fulfillment, until his eyes went watery with the effort.

And then one quiet night he knelt before God, satisfied. He held his beloved Old Testament in his left hand and his New Testament in his right hand, and he accepted Jesus Christ as his personal Lord and Savior.

Zimmie's life suddenly became very problematical, to say the least. He realized fully what persecution and suffering awaited him if he announced his newfound faith to his family and community. He fought with the decision, and he finally opted to leave Russia. One of the original missionaries who had testified to him suggested that he go to Hamburg, Germany, and report to Dr. Arnold Frank, a leading Hebrew Christian in Europe and a sympathetic dealer with such difficult cases. With a heavy heart but zeal for the Messiah, Zimmie left his homeland and went to Germany, a Christian without a home.

Dr. Frank, pastor of an Evangelical church and editor of a Hebrew Christian magazine called *Zion's Friend,* welcomed the new believer and immediately baptized him. Zimmie was now wholly committed to the service of the Lord.

The new Christian gathered himself together in Germany and set about writing a long letter of explanation to his father. He explained carefully everything that had transpired, why he had done what he had done, and that the matter was accomplished and closed. He explained why he thought Jesus Christ was the Messiah of the Jews, and he enclosed a New Testament for his father to study.

The elder Rabbi Zimmerman was not impressed; in fact, he was infuriated. By return mail came a letter ordering Zimmie to come home at once.

Zimmie could not do that, under the circumstances. He did not reply to the letter. Then came letters from his little sister and brother, both begging him to renounce this insane new faith and to return to them in Russia. Zimmie could discern teardrops on the pages, but he did not relent. The touching letters begged him to return at least to clear his name—to explain to the Jewish community that he was not a Christian and would never renounce his Judaism.

Zimmie sadly put the letters away and tried not to think about his family. He could not consider going home, and he resolved to find the best life he could as a spiritual orphan, knowing that God would guide him.

But Rabbi Zimmerman was not going to give up that easily. He determined to have his son back regardless what effort that took, and he traveled all the way to Hamburg to appeal to the young man in person. On the way he stopped at Berlin and enlisted the help and counsel of the chief rabbi of that great city. The two learned rabbis went forth on their mission, the "salvation" of a "former" Jew.

It was a dark, sad morning when Zimmie went to his door and found the two aged rabbis. His father looked stricken, the chief rabbi very grim. Rabbi Zimmerman was brief: "My son, my son, how can you be a Christian? Do you forget how the Christian people hate us, persecute us, and shed our blood like water throughout the centuries? How can you possibly do this?"

Zimmie asked the two to come in, and then he summoned all his patience and tried to explain what a true Christian was. A Christian believer would not and could not persecute the Jews or any other people he said. Jesus commanded that His followers love all men, and particularly the chosen people so beloved of His Father. He, Zimmie, was not in fact changing his religion or going over to some enemy; he was now simply a completed, fulfilled, New Testament-believing Jew, having obtained salvation through the Jewish Messiah and the Jewish New Covenant, he told them.

He got nowhere with them. They thought he was virtually raving. They had never heard such nonsense come out of the mouth of a Jew, not to mention a studied, devoted Jew as Zimmie had been. They would tolerate none of it, and they made that very clear.

At length Rabbi Zimmerman stated that he would make arrangements to use force, if necessary, to take his son home. Zimmie knew his father and understood that this was not an idle threat. He adopted a new tack. Part of the family was in America, in particular, Zimmie's older brother, Morris. Could the errant black sheep go there instead of back home to Russia? Zimmie appealed to his father to give his blessings on further traveling, solemnly promising to go straight to his brother's home upon his arrival in the United States.

Zimmie did not really want to undertake more travel, but he certainly feared the oppressive climate of his very Orthodox community at home. If his father were determined that he should return, perhaps the option of contending with his older brother in a new place would be better. Zimmie was unknown in America, of course; the community there, whatever it was like, would have no prejudices, he supposed, against a new immigrant.

Zimmie's brother Morris was an Orthodox Jew of the highest repute, cut from the same cloth as his father. Rabbi Zimmerman considered the alternative—perhaps his elder son could prevail upon Zimmie where he himself had failed. Perhaps the camaraderie between brothers would accomplish the reclamation of Zimmie. Perhaps Morris could bring this younger son to his senses.

And perhaps it would be a better thing to send this upstart, this thoughtless adolescent, off to a faraway land where he could provide no further embarrassment to his devoted family. After all, what if the young man were forced back to Russia and still refused to relent? There he would be among the devout, causing untold hardship for his family and their friends, and standing as an example to their entire city of a first-class *meshumed*—a "traitor."

The two rabbis consulted and finally agreed. Zimmie could go to the United States, directly to his brother's home in Long Branch, New Jersey, near New York City. He must go straight there, and abide there, without speaking to any sort of missionary or Christian along the way or after he moved in with his brother. Morris was to be entirely in charge of the affairs of Zimmie in America.

Before he left Hamburg and the kindness of Dr. Arnold Frank, the youthful pilgrim was given the address of a Jewish Christian medical missionary who lived and labored in New York City. But Zimmie was pledged not to contact the man, so he simply pocketed the address, planning never to refer to it. He thanked his friends of the Jewish Christian community in Germany and continued his travels, this time spanning the Atlantic Ocean to take on yet a new language and a new place.

It was good, in God's providence, that Zimmie came to America so early in his life. Some of his young German Jewish friends, the Christians among them included, were to end their lives in Hitler's camps much later, but Zimmie was, by his father's anger, freed of that curse.

Zimmie did not get a particularly warm welcome in New Jersey. Morris restated the rules of their relationship and did not hesitate to say what a burden Zimmie and his arcane beliefs would be in their very Orthodox household. Morris was definitely his father's son, dominating and fiercely committed to the Jewish Old Covenant ideals. He believed, as Rabbi Zimmerman did before him, that Christians were killers and that embracing their beliefs was tantamount to treason. Furthermore, Morris said, he would tolerate no mention of Christian doctrine in his household. He felt that his wife and children would be contaminated if Zimmie were to voice his beliefs.

Zimmie tried to live in the situation as it was outlined to him, but the relationship lasted only a week. Morris was simply unable to put up with the very presence of the apostate, as he thought of him, and ordered him out. Zimmie could go where he pleased in America, but he was barred from the home of his brother because of his faith in Christ.

This released Zimmie from his vows. If his brother could not abide his presence, then he was a free man, for better or worse. He was also a confused man, in a strange land, and not very experienced with life at his young age. Zimmie went to New York City, where he might find an opportunity to at least support himself. He had two dollars in his pocket.

The medical missionary was his only chance, and Zimmie went to his home. He was well received there, to his great relief.

From that point, Zimmie's American career for the Lord developed very rapidly. The missionary was stunned by Zimmie's testimony and felt that the young man deserved better. When Zimmie's English was adequate, he arranged for the youngster to attend Dubuque University in Iowa, and after three years of study there, Zimmie was better able to comprehend his new country.

Other brothers had immigrated by now, and Zimmie visited with them in Fort Worth, Texas. He witnessed boldly of his faith in Christ, being now much less the sacred immigrant or the overwhelmed young Christian than formerly. These brothers were somewhat more impressed with the sincerity of Zimmie's faith and more tactful than Morris had been earlier. Rather than cast out the errant Zimmie, they tried to interest him in their businesses. They could all live together somehow, after all, and Zimmie needed to get to work at something. Just being an educated American was not going to feed the Jewish Christian.

But Zimmie felt more and more driven to be of service to the Lord. His brothers were surely not going to come to Christ at this time, and if Zimmie went into their businesses he would amount to just another Jewish immigrant. No, he felt he had to make his faith better known among the Jewish community and among American Christians, so that all could see that the chosen people could indeed be saved.

On a shoestring, doing job work, Zimmie enrolled in Columbia Theological Seminary, one of the oldest and finest of American seminaries, connected with the Southern Presbyterian Church. He graduated with the bachelor of divinity degree and took up the pastoring of three very small Presbyterian churches in Georgia. It was a strange setting for a Russian Jew, speaking with his peculiar old-world accent, but Zimmie's heart was now full, and his service for the Lord especially zealous. His churches prospered, and his parishioners grew to love their unique pastor. Membership rolls grew, and buildings sprang up as Zimmie's ministry progressed. The Gentile Christians were seeing the effectiveness of one of God's chosen in the field. People were saved, and the small-town Georgians, who didn't know many Jews, were duly impressed by Zimmie's enthusiasm for the gospel.

During his seminary years, 1915-17, and later on during his pastorates, Zimmie had represented the Williamsburg Mission to the Jews, subsequently to become the American Board of Missions to the Jews. He spoke at churches on behalf of the mission and labored alongside the regular mission workers. He was a natural in this field of missionary work, of course, not only being a believing Jew in the flesh for all to see, but speaking Hebrew and Yiddish and having a complete knowledge of the Jewish law and Scripture. Few Jews could argue Judaism or Christianity with this scholarly representative of Christ, trained as he was both in Yeshiva and seminary. Zimmie was a powerful witness for Christ among his people.

The mission was eager to have his services, and Zimmie more and more felt called to the hard field of Jewish evangelism. At the end of the third year of his pastorates, Zimmie consulted with Dr. Leopold Cohn, himself an Orthodox rabbi and the founder of the Williamsburg Mission to the Jews. In prayer, he elected to join Dr. Cohn and his missionaries to the chosen people. He left his pastorates, in much better condition than when he had first come to them, and joined Leopold Cohn and his son Dr. Joseph

Hofman Cohn as a field evangelist for the mission. He did deputation work, speaking, and always one-on-one witnessing for Christ to the Jewish people.

Ironically, Zimmie had now become a Jewish missionary like those he had encountered in Russia, distributing literature, and never feeling bad when a tract was discarded in the street.

4

Out of the Wilderness

LOUIS LAPIDES

In America is a wilderness as desolate and ungodly as any to be found in the Jewish ghettos or the concentration camps of Europe. God is aware of it, and He sometimes calls His chosen ones out of that wilderness.

Louis Lapides "had it soft" compared to those heroes of the Old World persecutions, but his search for God and his final suitability as God's witness to the Jews is manifest in his remarkable testimony.

Louis is proof that God is not particular, not a "respecter of persons." He calls whom He will and from wherever He wishes. And though few might ever have dreamed that a muddleheaded drug addict of Sunset Strip would one day direct one of the largest Jewish mission efforts in the Western world, God had His special plans for Louis Lapides.

He was brought up on the East Coast in a Jewish community that carefully nurtured its own. That Louis was prepared for the reckless adventures that lay before him in his young years is very doubtful. That the Jew in general is up to the challenges of life that have always befallen

LOUIS LAPIDES (March 27, 1947–) is missionary-in-charge of the Los Angeles branch of the American Board of Missions to the Jews.

this peculiar people is a guarantee of God, however. The youngster was started out on a right and proper Jewish road through life with much early training and many admonitions from his community and synagogue.

He was to go through the valley of the shadow of death, but which of us does not, in his own way? He was to seek God in strange ways and strange places, but so have many others. He was to prove to be God's good servant in the end, and is that strange for the Jew? Has not God called this people to bless the world in His name?

Louis Lapides wanted to practice his bar mitzvah speech. Standing in the main sanctuary of the temple, he was all alone. Six years of study and preparation in Hebrew school at the ultraconservative New Jersey temple gave Louis's rather childish voice an added dimension.

But in spite of his forthcoming manhood and the solemn tone of his youthful voice, Louis was still a curious twelve-year-old. He spied a button on the sanctuary floor and stepped on it.

Much to his surprise, the doors of the ark began to open. Trembling with fear, the startled young man suddenly felt like Moses standing before the burning bush. Surely God would "sizzle" him on the very spot where he stood. Quickly he hid his eyes because God's own glory and holiness seemed to be revealed when the ark containing the Torah scrolls was opened. To be "sizzled" for such imprudent curiosity was a very real possibility, he thought.

But God had other plans for Louis. Louis continued his preparation for his bar mitzvah and the incident went undiscovered. However, he maintained a healthy distance from the button on the sanctuary floor from then on and counted himself fortunate to have escaped the personal attention of the God he loved and worshiped so dearly.

At last the long-awaited bar mitzvah arrived. It was time for Louis to stand before his God, no longer a child but in the full dedication of his manhood. It was a day of putting away childhood and coming of age.

The Jewish youth would have been surprised to have found this transition described in elegant simplicity in, of all places, the New Testament: "When I was a child, I spake as a child, I understood as a child, I thought as a child: but when I became a man, I put away childish things" (1 Corinthians 13:11).

However, the New Testament writer understood this coming of age well; he was a Jew. But on the eve of his bar mitzvah, Louis Lapides, a Newark, New Jersey, Jew of the twentieth century, had yet to encounter the writings of Paul or those of any other Hebrew Christian. Indeed, so had his family and relatives who swarmed about with excited congratulations and praise.

The celebration was complete; a new son had entered into the covenant with Abraham and Moses. The occasion was made even more joyous as the rabbi asked Louis if he wanted to continue his relationship with God and his training in Judaism. Louis answered boldly. Yes! Standing surrounded by his family and a host of well-wishing relatives and friends, he knew what was expected of him.

But, although his answer was bold and his voice strong, Louis's heart was troubled. How could he give his life to a God he did not really know? he wondered. He wanted to tell his rabbi how he felt, but standing in front of his proud and loving family, he could not express his nagging doubts.

As a child, Louis had associated the rabbi with God so

strongly and to such an extent that he had overwhelming desire to kiss him. If he kissed his rabbi, he felt, he would be kissing God.

But now he was no longer a child, and he knew that no matter how many times he kissed his rabbi, he still would not get any closer to God.

He ached for an intimate, personal knowledge of God, but on the very day of his dedication, God seemed more remote and aloof than ever before. The more Louis studied, the more he questioned his relationship to God. Failure to obey perfectly God's law frustrated him.

For Louis, it was a never-ending battle to acquire forgiveness for his sins, since he knew the Scriptures certified the Levitical ordinances of sacrifices as the only way to be forgiven. *Would the law ever be satisfied?* he wondered.

How could he know a holy God personally, as long as he could not meet perfectly God's demands? The very perfection of God's nature required human perfection, and Louis gained little comfort in his "atonement" for his sins. Was it really enough? It was not for him to change the Word of God, and yet he knew the law separated him from the very God that he wanted to know and love.

The love for God that had grown in Louis as a tenderhearted child had already begun to wither. Doubt and frustration plagued him. God had become remote and unreachable.

Louis knew his Jewish training had taught him the way to God was through prayer, charity, and good works— *mitzvahs.* Yet, this seemed to be inconsistent with what the Scriptures taught.

Unable to accept the inconsistencies between his training and the Scriptures, he lost all belief in the tenets of Judaism. Because he could not resolve his dilemma, Louis

Lapides, who had in childish adoration wanted to kiss God, now doubted His very existence.

Without God he would have to manage on his own, and Louis resolved to do so. Life was not so very bad, and for the most part he could not complain.

At eighteen years of age, Louis had everything under control. He was a Jewish American in a land of plenty. The grim reality of war belonged to another, older generation.

Born in 1947, Louis could not relate to the horror of death and destruction witnessed by Josef Herschkowitz or Elias den Arend. Such things were history and simply not a part of Louis's experience or life-style.

However, Vietnam was to become a part of his experience and life-style. The receipt of his draft notice in 1966 had been unexpected. But the Jewish teenager from Newark packed his bags along with a thousand other youngsters. War no longer belonged only to an older generation, and Louis was to get a front-row seat in the main event, courtesy of the United States Army.

When Louis was ordered to go to Vietnam, he was not too worried. He had been trained as a marine engineer to maintain amphibious craft and small boats. His job would not call for combat duty. In fact, he took the news of his assignment in a war zone very lightly.

War had never been a reality to Louis; it had been too easy to tune out. He could, as many Americans did, simply turn the dial of his television set to another channel as casualty reports or newsreels flashed across the screen.

Vietnam turned out to be inconvenient for Louis, but there was no threat of being singled out because he was a Jew, no special treatment reserved for a son of Abraham. It was a rather impersonal war in general, and it had not occurred to Louis that he could be killed quite impersonally by a stray bomb.

In a war zone, bombs are not labeled "for combat personnel only," and Louis's noncombat status would prove to be of little merit toward his survival. This thought occurred to him as he watched the "lightning" flashing below his plane, during its approach to the Saigon air field.

"It's only heat lightning," one of the men on board commented. But Louis frowned as he thought, *Since when does lightning come from the ground!* The flashes, of course, were bombs.

Suddenly, Louis realized God just might come in handy during the next year. As swiftly as the realization came, it was gone. It had been only a moment's faith, quickly forgotten as the troop carrier touched down safely.

Louis was not ready for the suffering and death that surrounded him. Army life was dreary and bleak, and the ugliness of war was something he was unprepared for.

God was an occasional thought fleeting through the chaos of war from time to time but not to be seriously examined by this Jewish boy turned atheist. Smoking marijuana eased the pain of coping, and for Louis it was more accessible than God.

Being Jewish, however, was an added bonus to relieve the monotony of work details on Friday nights or Saturday mornings. Louis often attended worship services. At last being Jewish was a plus.

Still he knew, in spite of his outward rejection of God, his survival was not a coincidence. He would be stationed in one area for a considerable period, only to be hastily relocated. Later he would learn the area had been bombed level within minutes after his departure. This happened time and again.

Maybe the holy God of Israel does come down from Mount Sinai once in a while, he thought.

Perplexed by the tranquility he often observed in the Oriental people in the midst of utter butchery and destruction, Louis began to investigate their culture and religions. At this point, it did not matter to him if he were to find God on Mount Fuji instead of on Mount Sinai.

On leave in Thailand and Japan, Louis intensified his efforts to find a means to God. The void within his own being drove him to search, but his focus was unclear and bent toward the mystical. Marijuana, Hinduism, Buddhism, and eastern philosophies had started to ease the vacuum he felt, but total satisfaction and fulfillment still eluded him.

Louis ended his twelve-month tour in Vietnam, searching and confused. He had spent the major portion of his time as a youth and now as a man in search of a God he had lost even before he found Him. Judaism had been his bridge to the Father, but in its uncertainty Louis had lost his way. Judaism and God had been one and the same to him; both were now doubted and rejected.

The inconsistencies of his religious training with the Scriptures had fortified his doubt, but now his own hunger drove him on to search; perhaps there was another bridge.

After his discharge, Louis moved to "swinging" southern California. He studied photography at the Los Angeles Art Center College of Design and obtained a job as a cameraman in a graphic arts studio.

Los Angeles, that melting pot of cults and exotic religions, provided a laboratory for an already confused Jewish boy from Newark via Saigon. The "City of Angels" afforded a generous sampling of seances, Satan worship, and scientology. It was the hub of cultism and almost any other "ism."

Louis continued his study of Buddhism and practiced disciplinary exercise as well as meditation. But no matter how involved he became in pagan religions, he knew that something just was "not kosher." His Jewish roots were deep. He was aware that his own Jewish God was far different from the gods of these other religions.

Los Angeles provided more than strange religions; it was the center of far-out life-styles and the mother of the drug scene. Louis searched for a holy God in the midst of paganism and drugs. He devoured all Los Angeles had to offer. But the more he "ate," the more hungry he became.

Brooding and alone, aided by hallucinogenic drugs, Louis concluded in a haze of mystical reasoning that if he could not find God, he must *be* God. Standing on Sunset Strip, Louis demonstrated his "divine powers."

It was there that the Reverend Barry Wood first saw Louis. Pastor Wood was not shocked by Louis's claims of divinity. Sunset Strip was his area of ministry; daily he encountered the bizarre, in the name of Jesus Christ. Louis was a routine customer.

Surrounded by a group of Christians one day, Louis was challenged to create a rock, if he indeed was God. Louis readily complied. Hallucinating, he held out his hand for all to see the rock he had created. The rock was created in his own mind, and only Louis perceived his creation.

"When God performs a miracle, it is for everyone to see and verify," he was told.

Even in his mystical haze, Louis realized he was a very small god indeed who needed drugs to experience his own divinity. His self-exaltation was exhausted, and he listened quietly.

Pastor Wood explained that he believed in Jesus Christ because He was the Jewish Messiah, and his proof was in the Jewish Scriptures. Then he proceeded to show Louis the Bible.

Louis "saw red." He had studied the five books of Moses as a child. What was this Gentile doing with his Jewish Bible?

Louis waited for the "Forty-second-Street hellfire and brimstone" message. It never came. Instead, Mr. Wood's manner and conservative style flowed with love and concern as he pointed out the prophetic Scriptures and explained his Messiah to Louis.

Louis only wanted to know what the God of Abraham, Isaac, and Jacob had to say about this Jesus. He would not read the Gentile book, the New Testament, but he did proceed to study the Bible from Genesis to Malachi.

For four months he poured over the Scriptures, alone, without the aid of a Bible commentary. Still heavily under the influence of drugs, his mind was foggy. But when Louis read the Scriptures, their meaning could not be obscured even by drugs.

His excitement grew as he studied the words of Moses. *What prophet could be greater?* he thought. He read Moses' own words in Deuteronomy 18:15. Speaking to the children of Israel, Moses had said, "The LORD your God will raise up for you a prophet like me from among you, from your countrymen, you shall listen to him" (NASB).*

Could Jesus be that prophet? Louis wondered. Psalm 22 and Isaiah 53 confirmed what he already suspected. Jesus was his Messiah.

He learned that the core of his problem was his own human nature. Righteousness, true and perfect, could be

New American Standard Bible.

found only in God. His own nature was not righteous. As he studied, he realized that what he had often felt in his school days was correct. No amount of discipline, study, self-will, or meditation could make him righteous before God.

Only Jesus met all the requirements prescribed by Levitical law. He was pure and righteous in the sight of God. In his sacrificial death, He gave the law that which it demanded—a blood atonement for the forgiveness of sin.

Louis realized Jesus was his bridge from the law to God, but still he held back. He wanted to be convinced, but the old habits of doubt were hard to break.

Louis compromised and headed for the Mojave Desert. God would convince him, he thought. He decided to help God with His revelation, and when he reached the desert he swallowed enough LSD for five people.

Only a real, living God could have broken through the darkness Louis experienced. Staring directly into the sun, he became temporarily blind.

As his mind began to clear, Louis literally saw his whole life pass before him. He suddenly knew God had not rejected him, not even now in the desert. He felt overwhelmed as his vision slowly returned.

In the face of God's grace, Louis knelt in the sand and prayed. "God, I blew it. I don't understand everything you want me to know about this Jesus, but whatever you want me to believe about Him, I do. You have shown me that Jesus is your Son and the Messiah of Israel, and that's enough for me."

In the next few weeks Louis noticed a number of changes in himself. He now had no psychological need for drugs; he felt a new, wondrous joy; he had a great desire to share his experience with God and with others. His co-workers noticed the change in him, too.

Louis was happy and content. The longing he had felt since childhood was filled. He no longer felt separated from his Creator; Creator and creation were one.

Louis reflected on his newfound contentment as he sat at lunch in a restaurant near the photography studio. He glanced about the room and was surprised to notice a familiar face.

The young woman acknowledged his greeting. Seeing that he was perplexed, she walked over, smiling. They had met before at a party, she reminded him, and her name was Deborah.

"Deborah," he repeated, back at work. He could not stop thinking about her, so he wrote a letter to a mutual friend asking her about the lovely Deborah.

The friend replied that Deborah was a Jewess who believed in Jesus. That was enough for Louis! He courted and married Deborah within a year.

Louis attended Deborah's church in Beverly Hills during their courtship. Their pastor was, of all people, the Reverend Barry Wood, the gentle, loving minister from Sunset Strip.

Pastor Wood announced one evening that his church would sponsor a three-day seminar presented by the American Board of Missions to the Jews. Louis was delighted. As much as he loved the Beverly Hills church, it was Gentile-oriented and hard to relate to his Jewish background. Now that he knew Jesus, the Jewish Messiah, he felt more Jewish than ever before.

Louis attended the seminar, and his excitement grew as he learned that there was a Hebrew-Christian fellowship throughout the world known as Beth Sar Shalom.

As sometimes happens with new believers in Christ, the direction of Louis's life began to change. He lost the great desire he had had for a career in photography. And he remembered his dedication to God at his bar mitzvah and his rabbi's questions. "Do you wish to continue your relationship to God, Louis? Do you wish to continue your studies?"

Yes, he thought. *Yes!* Louis was advised to go to Dallas Baptist College, a Christian liberal arts college in Dallas, Texas. So, one week after he and Deborah were married, they moved to Dallas.

The God of Abraham, Isaac, and Jacob claimed this son of His covenant, and Louis prepared for a full-time ministry.

Louis and Deborah were welcomed by the southwestern branch of the ABMJ and found a warm fellowship with Beth Sar Shalom in Dallas. Louis worked in the youth department of the Hebrew-Christian mission and started an evangelistic outreach program at one of the local high schools while he attended Bible college.

Over and over, Louis noticed a lack of Christian witnessing to his own people, the Jews. His concern grew. It seemed far too few felt the need to share the knowledge of the Jewish Messiah with the Jewish people.

He felt as Paul did when he said, "Brethren, my heart's desire and my prayer to God for them [Israel] is for their salvation" (Romans 10:1, NASB).

Understanding that his commitment to Jewish missions would require additional theological training, Louis returned to California to inquire about entering Talbot Theological Seminary in La Mirada, near Los Angeles.

During his visit, he met the Reverend Richard Cohen, who was at the time missionary-in-charge of the Los

Angeles Beth Sar Shalom. Louis spoke to him about part-time work with the mission while he attended Talbot Seminary. Mr. Cohen agreed, and Louis spent the next two years exploring the many approaches to the hard labor of Jewish evangelism.

He worked at the mission's literature table on the campus of the University of California at Los Angeles, sharing the Messiah with Jewish students. He studied the rabbinics and Jewish history in order to witness intelligently to the Orthodox Jews on campus. He was given the opportunity to speak at a variety of churches, locally and out of state. He spoke to Gentile believers about the Jewish roots of their own Christianity, the ungodliness of anti-Semitism, and how to witness to their Jewish friends.

Louis learned that being a missionary to the Jews required flexibility and involvement, a fact aptly demonstrated in door-to-door visitation, tract distribution, Bible studies, and personal counseling.

At the beginning of his third year with Beth Sar Shalom, Louis was asked to serve as missionary-in-charge of Greater Los Angeles. He was well prepared.

The once curious twelve-year-old who thought God would "sizzle" him on the spot as the doors of the ark slowly opened received the degree of master of divinity in Old Testament and Semitics from Talbot Theological Seminary in May 1976. At the time of this writing, he is continuing his studies at Talbot for another year in order to receive a master of theology degree in the same field.

God had other plans for Louis Lapides, indeed!

5

"There Goes Jesus!"

Hilda Koser

Hilda Koser is one of those American-born Jews with many missing ancestors. Her grandparents on her father's side and her uncles and aunts, save one uncle, were massacred on a Good Friday under the banner of the cross in Poland.

That was before her birth and in another country. But Hilda was made to remember it well. Her father knew Christians only as killers, from his upbringing in Poland after the Good Friday pogrom when his entire family, except for a brother, had been convicted as "Christ killers." He was never able to think of Christian people—or even of Christ, for that matter—as anything but murderers.

An Orthodox Jew, Hilda's father was stricken by the loss of virtually his entire family, and he left his empty home to become a ship's carpenter. He wandered from port to port, finally taking a job on a trans-Atlantic liner.

Hilda's mother was raised in Vilna, that fruitful city of Jewish orthodoxy. She, too, had an Orthodox background and suffered as the only daughter among twelve children.

Hilda Koser (November 24, 1914—) founded the Coney Island branch of the American Board of Missions to the Jews.

Though most young girls were not educated in that day, Hilda's mother profited by the knowledge passed along from eleven brothers and gained wisdom beyond keeping a kosher home and raising her own children.

At the age of fifteen, she went with a cousin to visit America. She was to return in one month's time, but on board the ocean liner she fell in love with the ship's carpenter. When the boat docked in Philadelphia, the marriage was arranged by her rather shocked American relatives.

Hilda was the third child, and by that time the family had moved to Brooklyn, where her father found employment in Williamsburg. Before Hilda's birth her father had become desperately ill. Doctor after doctor failed to render a diagnosis, but all agreed that death was very near. Seeking medical help in every possible connection, Hilda's father visited the dispensary in Williamsburg, which, unknown to him, was run by the Williamsburg Mission to the Jews, the forerunner of the American Board of Missions to the Jews.

The mission doctor came to the same conclusion. Mr. Koser was gravely ill, and the symptoms were too puzzling for accurate diagnosis. But the doctor reported to the missionary-in-charge, a Miss Sussdorf, saying, "That man will never live to get home. If you want to do something for God, go and see if he has a wife and children."

Missionary Sussdorf did exactly that and invited Mrs. Koser to the mothers' class being held at the mission.

"I could never go to a mission! I could never believe in Jesus!" said Hilda's mother. But she was impressed that the teacher was a former Orthodox rabbi, Leopold Cohn. Out of curiosity the mother agreed to go and took her three little children with her.

Things seemed to take a turn at that point in the life of the Koser family. It was discovered that Mr. Koser was suffering from tuberculosis, which, though barely treatable in those days, was at least an identifiable disease. He was sent off to a sanitarium in Coney Island for a complete rest, condemned to a virtual life sentence in a hospital room.

Mrs. Koser continued to go to the mission and learned to know and love missionary Leopold Cohn. Hilda recalls that the rabbi was "almost like a father to us."

Mr. Koser was "absent without leave" from the sanitarium at regular intervals, and within a few years there were five more Koser children resulting from his brief trips home. His illness lingered on as his family grew.

Finally, in the providence of God, Mr. Koser's illness seemed to abate, and he was allowed to return home from the sanitarium. Immediately he was approached by representatives of local Jewish newspapers who informed him that his wife had been bringing his family of eight children to the hated mission. They said they would help him gain custody of the children in order to prevent their conversion.

A court case was set up, and Mrs. Koser sent immediately for Leopold Cohn. Somehow Rabbi Cohn was able to persuade Mr. Koser to drop the charges, and the matter never quite came to custody litigation.

But the newly recovered father of eight was furious. There would be no further mission attendance for any of his family.

The children tried to maintain their attendance at the mission and received severe beatings. One by one, they stopped going. Finally, Hilda was the only one to attend the regular services. At age fifteen she accepted Jesus Christ as her personal Savior.

That summer Leopold Cohn sent Hilda to a Christian camp, and there she was called by God to become a missionary to the Jewish people.

Mrs. Koser had by this time also come to know the Messiah, but mother and daughter together had to maintain careful behavior around the volatile head of the family.

On Hilda's first night home from camp, she looked forward to kneeling to read her Bible and have her devotions. She had been taught at camp this way of approaching God and had gained great peace through the method. But she was caught by her father. Mr. Koser beat his daughter cruelly with a wooden coat hanger, screaming, "How could you believe in a Jesus that killed your grandmother, your grandfather, your aunts, and your uncles?" The tearful young girl tried to explain to her father that those who had done this terrible act could not have been believers in Jesus, for had he not taught, "By this shall all men know that ye are my disciples, if ye have love one to another"?*

Mr. Koser was too full of anger and too full of memories for an argument. He rejected his daughter in disgust.

When Hilda recovered from that terrible beating, she told the Lord firmly that it was going to be too much for her to be a missionary—the cost was too high. "If I would have to be beaten like that, I didn't want to be a missionary," she reports sincerely. "I told the Lord I would graduate from high school and support any missionary he wanted to send, but I would not go myself.

"The Bible tells us, 'Whom the Lord loveth he chasteneth,' "† reports Hilda with a sigh. Everything in her life seemed to fall apart when she withdrew her promise from the Lord, until finally one day she cried, "Lord, wherever you lead me, I'm willing to go."

*John 13:35.
†Hebrews 12:6.

The Lord opened the way for her to attend the Bible Institute of Pennsylvania, now known as Philadelphia College of the Bible. When she told her mother that she felt this was the leading of God, Mrs. Koser trembled and asked, "What will your father say?"

"I have to follow the Lord, Mother," Hilda replied simply.

When the news went through the family, Hilda's brother said, "It's your life. If you want to throw it away, go ahead."

Then it was time for Hilda to tell her father. She did so in simple terms. He replied that if she went to Bible school, he would never speak to her again. And he virtually never did.

Hilda sums up her Bible school education in a single Scripture. "At Bible school I learned to 'study to show thyself approved unto God, a workman that needeth not to be ashamed, rightly dividing the word of truth.' "‡ She never asked the Lord where He wanted her to go next, knowing that she was still called to be a missionary to the Jews.

After her graduation, Hilda was assigned by Dr. Cohn to Coney Island, where the mission had just purchased a new building in an Orthodox neighborhood. There were many children in the streets, and the area was composed of 95 percent Orthodox Jews. Hilda was grateful for the challenge.

Hilda was to stay nearly forty years in Coney Island, doing the difficult work of the mission among the Orthodox Jews. The beginning years were the hardest. She was like a traitor in their midst. And the mission remained a symbol of European Christian brutality among the first-generation American Jews. It was not so much that they rejected Jesus,

‡2 Timothy 2:15.

or even that they understood the gospel at all; they had seen what they assumed to be Christians in action, and they all had had enough "testimony" to last them a lifetime. It was thankless, plodding, discouraging work, but Hilda, led of the Lord, seemed to thrive on it.

Hilda concentrated on work among the children, whose minds were not poisoned against things non-Jewish. She held classes and patiently taught the gospel despite objections from parents and the community on every side. Her heart went out to these little ones who soaked up the gospel thirstily and were not at all understanding of their parents' opposition.

Like almost any of her pupils, Hilda suffered at home for her faith. She still lived with her parents, but her father never again used her name. "He never did call me 'Hilda' again. He called me 'Jesus.' If I sat at the table, and I wanted something passed to me, he would say, 'Pass this to Jesus.' If he saw me on the street, he would say to our Orthodox neighbors, 'There goes Jesus,' " Mr. Koser's cynicism toward the gospel knew no end, but Hilda bore her cross patiently.

"At first I cried over this," she reports. "But then I realized that if I were Jesus to my father, I would have to live differently from the other members of my family. I might be the only Bible my father would ever read."

Hilda's heart was broken when her father died without abandoning his cruel sarcasm toward her. She had never had a real chance to talk with him about the gospel. But after the funeral some of the neighbors, Orthodox Jews, came to her and said, "We must tell you what your father said about you. He said you lived what you believed, and that if it weren't for what happened in Poland to his parents and family, he would have believed, too."

Hilda holds to the promise of Acts 16:31, "Believe on the Lord Jesus Christ, and thou shalt be saved, and thy house," and hopes to see her father in heaven.

"He was alone in his bedroom," she says, "and there was evidence that he had gotten out of bed and back into it again before leaving this life. I have always held to the hope that at the very end he talked with the Messiah. He cannot possibly have been ignorant of what I believed, and he cannot possibly have failed to see what it did for me."

Hilda's work with the mission mainly took the form of Sunday school classes for the children, in which she showed the magnificent types of Christ in the Old Testament. There were many instances of strenuous objection, but Hilda holds precious the saved souls that resulted from such arguments.

Once when she was teaching a women's class about Christ, using the Psalms, three neighborhood ladies entered. They had come to break up the meeting with constant interruptions. Hilda told them firmly that they would have to be quiet while she taught, and that if they had questions afterward, she would deal with them. She was approached after the class by a Mrs. Feidel, who read Hebrew. Hilda opened a Hebrew Bible and asked Mrs. Feidel to read Isaiah 53—the suffering servant prophecy so clearly applicable to Christ. "Of whom is the prophet speaking?" Hilda asked Mrs. Feidel. There was no answer. Then Hilda offered Zechariah 12:10, and when she read, "They shall look upon me whom they have pierced," Mrs. Feidel jumped to her feet. "That's not in the Jewish Bible!" she declared.

Hilda told Mrs. Feidel to take the Bible with her and compare it with her own Jewish Bible at home. And she challenged Mrs. Feidel, "If that Scripture is not in the

Jewish Bible, then don't come back. But if it is—if you
find it in your Bible—then come back and bring your two
little boys with you." Mrs. Feidel agreed to the terms and
went home to study the Word of God.

She was back the following week with her children and
her admission that the Hebrew Bible used by the mission
was accurate. It wasn't long before she accepted Jesus as
her Messiah.

A Mr. Muslin showed up at an evening meeting following his son's attendance at one of the mission Bible clubs.
Mr. Muslin was not given to complex and subtle argument
about Scripture. He listened quietly to Hilda's Bible lesson and then approached her afterwards, saying, "Miss
Koser, I am a postman. I've delivered mail to a lot of
churches and Christian organizations. But no one ever told
me Jesus was for the Jews. I was a patient once in a Christian hospital. The chaplain would come around to see
everyone, but when he saw I was Jewish, he would just pat
me on the head and move on. My daughter was in a Girl
Scout troop that was held in a Christian church. Nobody
I met in that church ever told me Jesus was for the Jews.
But tonight, everything I ever heard in my lifetime fits together like a jigsaw puzzle. I want to accept the Messiah,
Jesus, as my Savior."

Not only did he receive Christ that night, but his wife,
son, and daughter did, too. It was an answer to Hilda's
longstanding prayer that she would see an entire Jewish
family come to Christ.

In dealing with the Jewish people, tragedy is always an
important issue. If Hilda had been able to show a life
among the believers free of such agonies as Jews typically
endured, then Christ would soon have become a shining
light in the community. But Christians have their trage-

dies, too. One believer in Christ lost a baby, a child of her later years. The baby died at birth, and the Christian woman was completely overwhelmed. "Why did the Lord permit it?" She sobbed. Hilda could only say, "This is His will."

The woman cried for six months for her lost baby, until her doctor confided to Hilda that she was nearing a breakdown. Hilda had to find a way to do something for her. The very idea of a stricken Jewish Christian woman in the community was enough to invalidate the word of Christ among the Jews. And the sorrow Hilda felt was all the worse because of the opinion of those who faulted the mission and its doctrine.

Most people counseling a woman in such a situation would commiserate, but Hilda felt led to continue to present the Word of God. She went to the still-tearful woman and said, "Betty, if you only want good from the Lord, you really don't belong to Jesus. He said, 'In the world ye shall have tribulation.'§ Job said, 'The LORD gave, and the LORD hath taken away; blessed be the name of the LORD.'‖ If you can't say the same, Betty, I doubt that you really know Christ."

The woman was shocked, of course, but she broke down right then and yielded even this problem to the Lord. She went home, washed her face, and pulled out of her rut.

Unknown to Betty, one of her neighbors had been watching her. The depressed Mrs. Domb had lost her husband and had been pining for him for several years. She wanted to see how Betty would handle her loss. When she saw the remarkable turnabout, Mrs. Domb came to Beth Sar Shalom. "I want the God who can overcome trage-

§John 16:33.
‖Job 1:21.

dies," she said. She now knows the greatest of all friends, Jesus, the Messiah. Hilda believes God answered Betty's prayer to use her baby, a prayer made before the stillbirth, and that is why He took the child to heaven. Through Betty's reaction to the tragedy, another Jew was brought into God's kingdom.

So goes the dramatic work of witnessing to the Jews in the Orthodox community. Though she began as an outcast, even in her own home, Hilda's total dedication to the Lord has made its mark among the Jews around the Coney Island mission.

The years have changed the look of the community now. Many of the Orthodox have passed on, leaving a painful earthly existence behind, and two new generations have become the flock of the mission. Through it all, Hilda Koser has stood by her post, continuing to teach her classes, comfort the followers of the Messiah, and confront skillfully the legion of objectors to the gospel of Jesus Christ. The singular incidents that describe the hostility of the Jewish people toward the Messiah, and the miraculous salvations of souls, go on and on through the lengthy and distinguished service of this dedicated missionary.

Some of the original children have grown up, gone through Bible school, and are in service to the Lord in many ministries. A portion of these serve in other installations of the American Board of Missions to the Jews throughout the nation and the world. Each of them now can supply his own stories of battles fought and won for Christ among the Jews.

Hilda sums up her decades of service to the mission and the Lord very simply: "I never asked for an easy place, and God did not give me one. All I can say is, great is His faithfulness."

6

Only Two Words

Sanford Mills

Dr. Sanford Mills, teacher, author, lecturer, and senior field evangelist for the American Board of Missions to the Jews, was born and raised an Orthodox Jew. His father was a very successful cheese manufacturer and exporter, and the family lived on its own estate in Russia-Poland. With the coming of the First World War, life fell apart for the Mills family, which began to move from country to country to escape the ravages of the war and the persecution of the Jews. They settled in Chelm, Poland.

Only the Nazis would outdo the Poles in persecution of the Jews in Eastern Europe.

Dr. Mills does not belabor the point but sums up his early experience in Poland: "There were killings, rapings, beatings, lootings, hunger, torture, regardless of age or sex."

The family gave up on the old country in 1921 and emigrated to the United States. Sanford was immediately enrolled in Hebrew school in an Orthodox Jewish community.

Sanford Mills (August 25, 1910-April 1, 1978) founded the Washington, D.C., branch of the American Board of Missions to the Jews.

His confused boyhood in Europe behind him, he settled
down to serious study of his faith. Not a breath of the gospel was heard in that neighborhood, and Dr. Mills today
deplores that. "We never heard the gospel," he says, "nor
did I ever hear of such groups as Hebrew Christians or
Jewish missions, although there was and still is a Jewish
mission in Cleveland."

The family was very strictly Orthodox; Sanford's father
attended synagogue three times a day and kept all holy
days. The family observed every feast and fast in Judaism.

At the age of fourteen Sanford left his Hebrew studies,
primarily because a change in schools revealed that the
scholarship varied with the rabbi. His last rabbi was a
Conservative and had contradicted some of the teachings
of his former Orthodox rabbis.

Then began Sanford's fifteen-year quest for the truth
about God. He discussed religion with any number of
people of various faiths. "Yet during all those years I *never*
heard the gospel," he said later.

In 1939 Sanford, now married, opened a small shoe store
in a nearby Ohio city. It happened that he hired a young
Christian clerk, a true believer, and a two-word testimony
of this solid Christian was to change the life of his em-
ployer, Sanford Mills.

> During this time I kept noticing something different about
> him. I asked him one day, "What in the world makes you
> so different from all the other Christians that I have met?"
> His reply was, "Jesus Christ." I proceeded to tell him
> what Jesus Christ meant to me. He then told me who
> and what was a Christian. To me, as a Jew, all Gentiles
> were Christians. I had *never* before heard the difference
> between a Gentile and a Christian. A week or so later, he
> and his wife and my wife and I went to a small Baptist

church where we heard two representatives of the ABMJ. One of them, Oscar Wago, spoke to me and gave me some Bible references to look up. When we came home, we looked up those references he had jotted down, such as Psalm 22; Isaiah 9:6-7; 52:13—53:12, and so on. A short six weeks from the time George Cochenour said to me, "Jesus Christ," we were baptized in a local Baptist church.

Mrs. Hannah Wago, presently retired from the ABMJ, but still active in the work of the Mission, made a number of trips to our home by bus from Columbus, Ohio. She was teaching us truths relating to doctrines: the second coming, the deity of Christ, eternal security, and others. These truths formed the basis for my faith all these years. How we thank the Lord for her faithfulness.

Later on that year, the newly saved Millses were invited to Columbus for a Bible conference and to meet Dr. Joseph H. Cohn, then president of the ABMJ. At the conference Dr. Cohn asked Sanford Mills to give his testimony. It was a routine request, but in the case of Sanford Mills one that was terribly hard to fulfill.

In those days Sanford stuttered whenever he faced a group and had done so virtually since learning to speak. He had never been called on to speak or recite in schoolrooms and had always avoided public speaking. He informed Dr. Cohn of his disability, in the manner of Moses informing God of the same, but Sanford Mills did not have a brother to speak for him. Dr. Cohn, when he was introduced, called on Sanford anyway.

Sanford approached the platform, saying to the Lord, "If I stutter, never again will I consent to speak in public." He whispered to Dr. Cohn, "I think I'm going to make as big a fool out of you as I will of myself."

Prayerfully, he took his place at the rostrum, opened his mouth, and began to give his testimony.

It may have been a small miracle, as Christian miracles go, to the people who were in attendance that day. But Sanford Mills did not stutter on that evening and never stuttered again before a crowd for the rest of his life. His work now, in the providence of God, requires almost constant public speaking to huge audiences.

Dr. Cohn was visibly moved by the testimony of Sanford Mills at that conference. A month later he contacted Mills, asking him to become part of the ABMJ. "I was amazed," Sanford recalled. "It was my friend Mr. Wago who had spoken to Dr. Cohn on my behalf and without my knowledge. Because of my training and background, my dear friend concluded that I would do much better not selling shoes but helping bring the gospel to my people."

It was a difficult decision for an immigrant really still adjusting to a new society, and having only just made a successful start in business, to become a Christian missionary But a few months later Sanford and his wife prayerfully accepted the call of the ABMJ and joined the mission in 1940. "We went from the *sole* business to *soul* business. What a change!"

> Now we began a series of studies refreshing my Hebrew, learning Jewish apologetics, attending classes at the Bible institute, as well as practical training, preaching, witnessing, street meeting, etc. Also studying months on end with private teachers supplied by the mission. Homework was greatly intensified, which kept me up until the wee hours of the morinng. Mrs. Mills typically sat on the opposite end of the table with an English Bible while I was reading and translating from the Hebrew Bible. What training! What discipline!

The Mills family's first call was to Washington, D.C., where Sanford and his wife began a mailing program using *Shepherd of Israel,* one of the ABMJ publications still in issue. Within six months their outreach included hundreds of Jewish families, and after a year they were in steady contact with seven hundred Jewish households. They called on the Jewish community daily, receiving many rebuffs and, with some, gaining a certain grudging acceptance. Many nights they did not return home until two or three o'clock in the morning, after exhausting discussions over the Scriptures with Jews who were making a serious search for God. Sanford recalled:

> Our first convert was less than six months after we came to Washington. One evening we came into a Jewish home and one of the family's friends was also present. The father in this home was a convert to Judaism. We were there over five hours discussing the claims of Jesus as the Messiah of Israel. Seemingly we got nowhere.

But a few days later they received a telephone call from the onlooker. Her request was for the Millses to go and get her husband from the tubercular sanitarium. Sanford agreed on one condition—that she would not reimburse him for the expense. She consented.

The next day Sanford and Mrs. Mills, went out to the sanitarium and picked up the very sick man. He had been a former theater organist, but now it was obvious his body had wasted away. Sanford drove very slowly, talking all the while about the prophecies relating to Christ the Messiah. He made an appointment to see the man the next afternoon. The evangelist realized he didn't have much time.

On the next afternoon the discussion was picked up exactly where they had left off. The sick man continued to want to know why Mills would go to such trouble for him, and who was going to pay the expenses. The evangelist told him that he merely wanted to share with him all that God had given, and since God had so much and asks for so little, why should the expenses come into question? In the course of their discussion, the organist said that he was too weak to go to church anymore or even to walk around. Mills patiently told him that it was not necessary to go to a church to receive the Lord Jesus—he could do that even in bed—and, like a child, the tuberculosis sufferer received the Lord Jesus Christ as his Messiah and Savior. He was the first convert of Sanford Mills.

There was some alarm over the fact that the patient was not able to eat anything. He could take only liquids and was becoming very weak. It had been five days since he left the sanitarium; it was decided to take him back where he could have complete rest and more treatment. The family was just finishing dinner, and the new convert asked Mills if he would help him to the organ in the living room of their home. The evangelist asked how he could play the organ, since he had not eaten for five days, but he said, "Just take me there; God will give me strength." And there, in the presence of his wife, son, and seventy-six-year-old mother, with the hands of a master, he played "The Old Rugged Cross." When he finished, he fell back into the arms of Sanford Mills, who carried him to the car and drove him to the sanitarium.

That very night, Sanford received a telegram saying that his father had died. It was sent by his wife's cousin since Sanford, now an outcast from his family, was no longer in touch with his parents. The Millses left early in the morning for Cleveland, paid their respects to the family, and returned home.

The telephone rang as they were entering the house; it was the wife of the new convert. Tragedy had struck in their absence, and they were asked to drive immediately to the sanitarium. They were too late; they arrived just as the mortician was carrying out the body of the organ player in a wicker basket.

The organist's wife related the story: The sanitarium had phoned, asking her to come at once. She took the bus immediately and found her husband in a coma. He had tubercular meningitis and was very near death. She sat at his bedside for two days, trying to talk to him, and watching him put his hand to his ear—as if he could barely hear her. At the end, he put his hands together and very softly said, "Thanks be to God and Jesus Christ that you are all right," and died. It was exactly seven days after he confessed the Lord that he went into His eternal presence.

It was difficult for Mills to enter Jewish homes on weekends. The Orthodox would not receive such a visitor on the Sabbath, of course, and ironically the less religious Jews were too busy on Saturdays maintaining their businesses to talk about God. Sanford tried to contrive a way to put his Saturdays to good use, and he got the idea of applying for a job in a Jewish-managed shoe store. In a short time, he had such a job and had struck up a friendship with the manager. Slowly, a relationship formed between the Mills family and the manager's family, until they began to regularly have lunch and dinner on Saturdays in each other's home after the store was closed.

The inexperienced evangelist thought he had to go very carefully and step-by-step with this business-minded and very practical Jew. One day he intentionally left his Hebrew Bible in the store during a coffee break. Returning in about an hour, he noted that the manager had indeed leafed through the Bible.

The following Saturday, the manager had some questions about the Scriptures, and this led Sanford to provide him with a number of tracts written for the Jews by the ABMJ. He actually asked the manager's opinion on the quality of the tracts, requesting him to tell him what he thought of the messages—whether they might be effective, offensive, or whatever. Sanford had to wait a week between each witnessing session, of course, since he worked at the shoe store only on Saturdays.

During the Saturday after the manager had received the tracts, Sanford picked a moment when there were no customers in the store. "I asked him what he thought of the tracts. Did he think that Jesus was presented properly? I asked for his candid opinion. He was very much impressed. 'Very well done,' he said.

"I then said, 'Jack, since this is your estimation of the literature, what are you going to do with Jesus Christ?' To my amazement and joy, he replied, 'What am I going to do with Jesus Christ? Why, I am accepting Him as my Messiah, my Lord, and my Savior.' "

Mills was overwhelmed by the ease of this conversion. The tracts themselves seemed to have done the whole job. The evangelist humbly claimed no credit. "Jack" was his second convert in Washington, D.C., in less than nine months, and like his spiritual mentor, Sanford, Jack closed his shoe store and went into full-time service for the Lord, becoming a missionary in Washington.

The doors of the churches in Washington were beginning to open to the Millses, and the Jewish community became aware of their work. One of the key difficulties of

Jewish missions is that churches have an apathy toward witnessing to Jews and that Jews have somehow become the last, rather than the first, to receive the gospel of Jesus Christ (see Romans 1:16). There are even churches who object to Jewish evangelism and some who hold doctrines that deny the Jews the worship of their own Messiah. But the Millses were able to overcome the objections, and diplomatically they cultivated the Jewish community as well as the Christian churches.

Rabbis called on Sanford, asking for an audience. No one seemed to become angry with him. One rabbi even came to a church to hear him speak. The former stammerer, nervous before a crowd, had become a compelling speaker for the Lord. Evangelist Sanford Mills counted Jewish rabbis among his personal friends, saved and unsaved.

At one point, Sanford was asked to speak to a Jewish women's group, but he declined on the grounds that he would have to have the local rabbi's consent to his appearance. This seemed to increase the respect of the Jewish people for his work.

On the other hand, subtle Jewish objections were expressed in friendly ways. Several Jewish businessmen, attempting to get Sanford to leave his mission work, tried to tempt him with lucrative offers, but the evangelist persevered for the Lord, cultivating friend and foe alike.

Some of the Washington churches noted the remarkable but dependable phenomenon that when a Jew is saved in their midst, or by their witness, revival results as the Lord blesses. One particular church in Washington was to remain the special assembly of the Millses' mission even long after the missionaries left the city. Sanford and Mrs. Mills were moved out of Washington and back to Columbus,

Ohio, because of the leading of the Lord in that particular area and the need for a strong field evangelist, but Sanford returned to Washington on annual trips to share the needs of Jewish mission work with the churches there.

During one of these return trips, Christian friends introduced the Millses to a Jewish lady to whom they had witnessed energetically. Sanford and his wife took her out to dinner, talked to her for several hours, and in the course of that evening they led her to the Lord. On leaving the city, they urged her to go to the church their friends attended and make a public confession when the invitation was given. The Jewish woman did that, and the church and the pastor rejoiced.

The next year when Sanford returned, the pastor told him about the remarkable revival that had taken place in the church since that singular salvation. On each annual trip, that church held a Bible conference as a further expression of gratitude to the Millses. The ABMJ has invariably been welcomed in that church.

Unfortunately, the Jewish Christian woman did not survive long to see the revival she had inspired. A year later, she returned to her native Boston for a routine operation and died in one minute on the operating table, allergic to the anesthetic. A beautiful testimony was silenced, but the church and the Bible conferences go on in victory.

Back in Ohio, the field work began to spread amazingly as evangelist Mills received requests farther and farther from his home base. Finally, the requests came from over the Ohio borders, and the mission spread to Indiana, Michigan, West Virginia, and Pennsylvania.

At the beginning, Sanford was requested for single services in churches that realized Jewish evangelism was part of a valid Christian mission but that did not let the matter "get out of hand." But now, he began to receive requests for meetings of several days and several services, leading to complete seminars and conferences. One city after another opened to them, and before Sanford's death in 1978 they had returned to some churches for thirty-five annual conferences. The senior field evangelist covered a regular route stretching as far as Texas and Florida and through many states of the Union, where he held yearly meetings and urged witness to the Jewish people.

God has placed the Jewish people everywhere, and unlike a mission to the natives in the forests, say, or to the Eskimos, the Jewish evangelist has only to go anywhere in his own locale, and Jews will be found. Sanford Mills always went exactly where the Lord called, and his field became wider and wider as zealous churches continued to call him. Jews have been saved, memberships built, and blessings enjoyed in the wake of Sanford's steady teachings.

The sort of ministry pursued by Dr. Mills is essential to Jewish evangelism. If it were left to only Jewish Christians to propagate the faith, then each one would be terribly overburdened, and generally the ABMJ has only a few missionaries to confront an entire community. But if Gentile Christians will go out and witness to the Jews they know, then a new revival among the Jewish people will be more likely.

The ABMJ missionaries repeatedly emphasize that the Gentile Christian churches were originally founded by Hebrew Christian missionaries: Peter, Paul, John, James—all those of the New Testament. All the Lord's disciples were Jews, all the apostles were Jews, the original Christian church of Jerusalem was Jewish, and it was that church that sent missionaries to the Gentiles. Dr. Sanford

Mills and the other field evangelists of the ABMJ have gone from church to church, from state to state, from nation to nation, to remind Gentile Christians of the responsibility they have to the brothers of the Lord (Matthew 25: 40).

Dr. Mills grew accustomed to seeing people come forward for salvation, Jews and Gentiles alike, wherever he taught. Pastors are confounded by seeing Jewish people, attending for the first time, come forward in their churches. Sometimes the pastor has been in a church for twenty-five years and has never seen a Jewish salvation. Numbers of church people have never spoken with a Jewish person about God, though they know Jewish people in their work and in their neighborhoods. Once the pastor of a church in introducing Dr. Mills confessed that he himself had dedicated his life to the ministry during one of Sanford's previous Bible conferences.

In the ministry of Dr. Mills, as with any Jewish evangelist, the front-line stories of Jewish salvations are unusual. One he particularly treasured happened during a conference in Ohio. A young lady telephoned him repeatedly every evening. She seemed too timid to talk face-to-face, but, as a result of the phone calls, she dedicated her life to the full-time service of the Lord. But then there was a serious problem—she was in love with an unsaved premedical student. She began to witness to him and finally persuaded him to go to church with her one Sunday night. He still does not remember the message, but he was drawn forward during the invitation. How the Lord was working! Not only was he saved, but also he dedicated his life to the full-time ministry. He transferred to Baptist Bible College in Springfield, Missouri, graduated, and is now pastor of a church in Baltimore. What a comfort he

was to Dr. Mills when he joined him at the hospital while
Mrs. Mills was undergoing surgery.

Dr. Mills described in his own words some activities
that were typical of his entire ministry.

> The last month, as I write this chapter, has been one of
> the most rewarding, encouraging, and comforting periods
> in my ministry. When I came home recently from the
> hospital, my chiropractor asked us to contact a Jewish
> couple. He had witnessed to them for some time, but felt
> that a Jewish Christian testimony was necessary to bring
> them to a saving knowledge of the Lord Jesus Christ.
> They came to our home, and we spent three hours just in
> the Old Testament, presenting Christ to them. We saw
> them gloriously saved! The next day, Sunday, we walked
> down the aisle with them in public confession, and they
> were baptized three weeks later. Praise His name!
>
> That same week, I received a very heart-rending letter
> from a Jewish lady I had been asked to see some eight
> years before, when I was in St. Albans, West Virginia. As
> I read her letter, I recalled how I had driven to her home,
> but could not drive up her driveway as she lived on a hill,
> which at that time was covered with ice. Slowly, I strug-
> gled on foot up the driveway and into the house. As we
> sat down and began to talk, I knew she was listening with
> a closed mind. However, claiming a promise from God
> that His Word would not return unto Him void, I pursued
> in presenting Christ to her and left the house—half walk-
> ing, half sliding—to my car. I still claimed that promise,
> but felt it was wasted time.
>
> I had dismissed that experience, as I had a number of
> others, until I received her letter—a letter of heartbreak
> and struggle, but also eight years of preparation by the
> Holy Spirit. The woman asked if I remembered her, and
> the experience of that past evening (how could I have
> forgotten the long walk on that sheet of ice?!). She wanted

to know if I could forgive her for that evening, and told me of the many tragedies she had experienced during those eight years. She expressed her desire to recapture our visit of so long ago, stating that now she would listen—now, maybe, she could even see. She asked if it were possible to talk with me again and wanted to know when I would be in her area.

Mrs. Mills read the letter and wept. We were 1,200 miles from St. Albans, West Virginia. It would not be possible for us to visit the lady for at least six months. A few days later, I did the next best thing and telephoned her, telling her to forget the cost and talk as long as she wanted—the Lord would provide! We talked for approximately 40 minutes, thanking God for the telephone. The woman was certain that all of her problems and questions would be answered, if she could only see me. I asked her if I could send a friend of mine to her from a nearby city. He is an excellent pastor and a superb soul winner, having baptized over 1,100 Roman Catholics in his church. The Jewish lady consented to see him, but felt she still needed to visit with me.

I then telephoned Dr. Fuchs and asked him to arrange a trip to headquarters in New Jersey. I told him of my experience of eight years before, and read the letter to him. Dr. Fuchs was also moved to tears as he listened to the letter, and suggested that we go to see this lady after our meeting in New Jersey. I agreed, even though this would mean a long trip for Mrs. Mills and myself (and we had both been hospitalized only a short time before). I trusted the Lord to give us the strength for the task.

Our chiropractor read the Jewish lady's letter and wrote a check to the Mission to pay for some of the expense. Dr. Fuchs assured us that the Mission would pay the rest. Arrangements were made for the lady and her husband to meet us at the airport, and we were on our way!

During the trip, I wondered if I would recognize the lady when I saw her, but when we arrived, I recognized her immediately. We gathered together our luggage and got into her car. She began talking immediately as we drove to a nearby restaurant for lunch, and we continued to talk while we sat in the parking lot of the restaurant, waiting for it to open. After a half hour of talking and witnessing, she gladly, eagerly, and with tears running down her cheeks, confessed the Lord Jesus Christ as her Messiah and Lord. The change in her face, after a two-hour session in the restaurant, was amazing. They took us back to the airport, and we were on our way back home to Florida.

We came, we saw, and Christ conquered!

Dr. Mills kept busily at work in a still-expanding ministry after years in the field. Expenses for special trips were still paid by anonymous Christian donors; pastors still stood back in amazement as local Jews came up their aisles for salvation; and those mysterious late night telephone calls still came from searching Jews, asking to be shown the principles of the gospel in Old Testament prophecy. God still blessed the ministry of the elderly Dr. Mills and his wife, who continued to persevere for the gospel of Christ—invariably taking it to the Jew first.

Dr. Sanford Mills remained indebted to the young shoe salesman who first uttered to him the saving words that transformed his life: "Jesus Christ."

7

To the Jew First—And Also to the Nazi

EMANUEL LICHTENSTEIN

The testimony of Emanuel Lichtenstein, courageous ABMJ missionary in the Gestapo terrorized Vienna of early World War II, has been touched upon earlier. It was Lichtenstein who first confronted Josef Herschkowitz, the atheist of Dachau, and spirited him away to Holland.

It is difficult to imagine being called to a more hazardous ministry in all Christendom. Emanuel Lichtenstein operated fearlessly among the Jews of Austria while the Nazis were hunting them down. He testified of Jesus Christ even to the Gestapo themselves!

The material contained in this chapter was originally written by Lichtenstein himself, painstakingly in English, and sewed by hand with a thread binding. Brother Lichtenstein's English was only mediocre, but he was able to bring people to Christ in German, Swedish, and Spanish as well.

His memoirs begin with what well could have been his end—a call from the Gestapo in Vienna. It was 1942, a very late date for a Jew to be alive and free in the streets of that

EMANUEL LICHTENSTEIN (April 15, 1892–) founded the Buenos Aires branch of the American Board of Missions to the Jews.

hellish, occupied city, and it seemed that the missionary's number had literally come up. He who had saved so many from destruction had now caught the attention of the German overlords, and he was instructed to report to the *Geheime Staatspolizei* headquarters—virtually a death sentence in itself for a Jew. Few Jews entering the Gestapo headquarters ever came back out.

But this was a new sort of case for the police. Lichtenstein was a Christian missionary, after all, not an ordinary Jew. And yet he was thoroughly Jewish, too, and therefore subhuman. Just how subhuman he was remained to be determined by a personal interview.

The missionary was told to report immediately and had only time to grab a few documents attesting to his work in Vienna for the ABMJ. Whether these documents would have any special meaning to the Gestapo he did not know, but they at least showed that he had employment, and not, strictly speaking, at a synagogue.

Lichtenstein also grabbed the Christmas issue of *Das Auserwaehlte Volk (The Chosen People)* as he left his quarters. The issue featured a photograph of the missionary and his grandfather, Ignaz Lichtenstein of Hungary, the noted Hebrew Christian Orthodox rabbi.

(And thereon hangs another whole tale—the heroic ministry of Rabbi Lichtenstein, which occurred around the turn of the century. That singular soldier of Christ preached the New Testament from the Orthodox Jewish pulpit in Hungary. He was spat upon in the streets of the Jewish community, beaten, and generally regarded as the worst of traitors, but he stayed at his post until his death in 1909. A barber purposely disfigured his beard on one occasion, and he led the life of a criminal in the streets of his home city. When he died he was buried in a Reform, rather than an Orthodox, cemetery—as if this would strip him of his Orthodox credentials, and a cruel obituary ["May his name be blotted out"] was run in the local newspaper.

Now his grandson, also a follower of the Messiah, was to go on trial for his life before the Nazis.)

Missionary Lichtenstein was confronted by two Gestapo officers when he arrived at the dreaded headquarters office. They were aware of his special calling, he assumed, as they censored all mail in and out of the occupied Austrian capital. This private hearing would probably be a rubber-stamp matter; the missionary would likely be placed in a concentration camp and never heard from again.

But he was questioned carefully by an interrogator first. "What does mission mean?" his questioner wanted to know, and particularly, "mission among Israel."

Lichtenstein patiently displayed his documents, which explained his employment and his belief in Jesus Christ. The Gestapo agent studied the materials with a quizzical look, either having never known of a Jewish Christian or pretending that he had not. The second officer remained silent.

"You're a follower of 'the Lord Jesus Christ!'" the first officer suddenly shouted in Lichtenstein's face. *"What does this mean?"*

He shoved the photo of Lichtenstein and his grandfather under the missionary's nose, demanding to know what perversity this was. The caption was clear: *"Grossvater und Enkelsohn, beide Nachfolger des Herrn Jesu Christi"* (Grandfather and grandson, both followers of the Lord Jesus Christ). What seemed to frustrate the officer was the loophole nature of Lichtenstein's rather special Jewish calling. In the mind of the Nazi, Jews were Jews, not Christians. Killing Jews was his business; Christians might well be another matter. Some of the *German* people were Christians, obviously. Was this miserable, racially inferior rodent called Lichtenstein going to slip out of his grasp on a technicality?

Lichtenstein acknowledged his faith in Jesus and testified to the executioner in the bargain. "Nachfolger," he translated for the German, "means follower, and it refers to people of all nations who follow the Lord. He is our one and only Savior, who died for our own personal sins and those inherited by all mankind."

At that the second officer, the silent one, left the room. Lichtenstein did not know what meaning to attach to his departure, but he noticed that his examiner immediately took a different tone. He softened quite a bit, becoming almost mild. Perhaps the other had been the chief executioner, because he was now confronted with a much softer-spoken interrogator. Maybe his examiner had only been showing how severe he was with the Jews for the benefit of his superior.

Still looking at Lichtenstein's papers, the officer said quietly that he did not want to go into religious matters that he did not completely understand. Lichtenstein was dumbstruck; was he really going to slip through their fingers? The officer warned him to discontinue writing letters abroad, and he stamped a permit for leaving the building. Those permits were hard to come by, the missionary well knew.

And then that Gestapo officer made a perfectly remarkable statement to his prisoner: "And now get out quickly. *Go, in Jesus' name!*"

Lichtenstein did as he was told, gratefully. How good it was to see the sunlight again!

What had happened in the heart of that policeman who routinely dispatched the Jews to certain death? Had he a glimmer of faith of some kind? Did he fear God? Did he suppose that when God judges his deeds he will at least be able to say that he released one "follower of Jesus Christ"? Lichtenstein observes in his memoirs:

> I felt quite clearly that he did not say the words "in Jesus' name" ironically. I did not doubt that this man—usually personified cruelty towards innocent people—had been touched for just one single moment and became mild and soft on this occasion. Perhaps he became aware that on doomsday he would not find justification for having pursued a follower of Christ unjustly, unfairly, and without any reason at all.
>
> When I at last left the bars and gates of that horrible building, I breathed deeply and felt a great relief, thanking God for what he had done for me.

Lichtenstein notes a special thanks for *The Chosen People,* also. Without that magazine and that peculiar photograph showing him and his grandfather, the interrogation might have taken quite another turn. It was most unusual for a Jew to be allowed to answer to *anything,* let alone a question of religious gravity, once the Gestapo moved in. But the photograph had distracted them from the main business at hand—the virtual execution of Emanuel Lichtenstein—and the missionary was free again.

That for all practical purposes ended the Austrian career of missionary Lichtenstein. He felt obliged now to arrange for his own departure, through Stockholm, Sweden, and he came finally to Argentina in 1942. It had been a good four years or so since the Reich had taken over; however, many conversions and much in the way of good works for the Lord had been realized.

Lichtenstein and his family had come to Vienna as refugees from Hungary in 1937. They were welcomed by the then missionary to the Jews in Vienna, the Reverend Friedrich Forell, and summarily welcomed into the service of the ABMJ.

The major service at first was providing for the many refugees who poured penniless into Vienna. Soup kitchens were set up by the ABMJ, which served nourishing foods and the even more nourishing gospel of the Messiah to the wandering Jews of Europe. Relief funds collected in America were quickly dispatched for use in troubled Europe, and the missionaries fed the multitudes, even as the disciples had distributed the loaves and fishes.

Up to one hundred fifty starving people at a time would be accommodated in the ABMJ's soup kitchen, and the new missionary was able to report the salvation of numbers of Jews. Lotte Furth was saved; she was to go on to Bible school and to see service with the ABMJ in future years. Josef Herschkowitz was saved, of course, but Lichtenstein was not to know about this victory until many years later. The Jews became of necessity so far separated from one another that they might well all be working for the same mission and still not know of each other's salvation.

It becomes clear, as these dramatic stories of Jewish salvations continue, that God still works along faithful lines, as He did with the line of Seth and Shem. As a result of the pulpit of Rabbi Lichtenstein back in Budapest at the turn of the century, his grandson was saved. Through the witness of his grandson, Josef Herschkowitz was saved. Through the ministry of Herschkowitz in the United States and Lichtenstein in Argentina, countless others were saved. And they all continue to reproduce, steadily building a more potent Jewish witness for the Messiah. Dozens, hundreds, thousands—just as in the first century church—continue to reserve places in the Kingdom to come, where the Jews will at last live in perfect peace.

There exists among the private papers of Emanuel Lichtenstein a letter from Josef Herschkowitz, dated November 6, 1946 at Erie, Pennsylvania. It had been several years since Lichtenstein, who had first uttered the gospel message to Herschkowitz, had heard from the man he spirited away to Holland. Lichtenstein had not heard of the subsequent salvation of the former atheist, and so he was joyfully surprised.

The letter begins, "Greetings in the name of our LORD JESUS CHRIST. It will probably surprise you to get a letter from someone you do not remember." The letter continues with the testimony of Herschkowitz and his statement, so remarkable to Lichtenstein, "Now I am, since June 1, 1945, a full time worker and since June 3rd, 1946, an ordained Baptist minister working as an itinerant evangelist for the American Board of Missions to the Jews."

Herschkowitz goes on to inform his mentor that he never fails to mention Lichtenstein as the first one to present the gospel to him, and he concludes, "Now I am praying that the Lord may give you what I never could give you—all the desires of your heart and much more fruit. Thanking you for the way you have led me and asking the LORD'S continued blessings upon you, I am your co-worker for CHRIST, Josef Herschkowitz."

Lichtenstein's equally touching reply is dated February 8, 1947, in Buenos Aires (the mail traveled slowly by sea). "Even if I am used to seeing miracles happen in my daily experience, and even if it is true that especially the last (few) years have been packed with evidence of God's

working, I cannot but see one more miracle in your very
nice letter of Nov. 6, 1946."

He followed this with an extremely detailed updating
on the Vienna ABMJ work and on the work then going on
in Argentina.

And so it goes. We shall not know just what seeds that
we have sowed have fallen on good ground until we all
get to heaven. Jewish reunions will be especially joyful in
the presence of the Lord, since these are the people He has
chosen to scatter so widely that they lose track of each
other.

But to get back to the story of missionary Lichtenstein,
his departure from Germany was not comfortable. He had
been given a ticket to Stockholm, but he still had to clear
Nazi customs.

Like his grandfather before him, Emanuel Lichtenstein
had remained at his post until the final hour. On the day
the Nazis declared war on Russia, the mission was closed,
and the missionary was obliged to run for his life. The
precious air ticket to Sweden would get him out of Vienna,
but the plane had to stop in Berlin. Lichtenstein's passport
was marked with a big "J," standing for "Jewish," and his
middle name, according to Nazi regulations for all Jews,
was "Israel."

What sort of Nazis might he run into at customs? Would
he leave Vienna only to be detained in Berlin? Would he
end up in the gas chambers after all? Whether he be a
Gestapo overlord or a petty customs official, any Nazi had
the power of life and death over any Jew. Emanuel Lichtenstein approached customs in Berlin with trepidation.

He encounterd all he feared at the baggage-examining
counter.

An officer ordered him to open his trunk, and there, on

top of all his belongings, was a wooden cross. It had laid on his writing desk for many years. It was inscribed with the word *Sitio* ("I am thirsty").

"Why does a Jew need a cross?" the customs man began quietly. He had of course examined the wholly Jewish name and passport of this particular customer.

The missionary, trembling, began to explain the concept of Jews following Jesus, much as he had back at the Gestapo headquarters in Vienna. But this particular officer was in no way interested. He cut off the answer and ordered a body search of Lichtenstein.

This was critical. It would take time. The plane might leave, and Emanuel had no idea how he would schedule another or even if he would be permitted an alternate departure.

But somehow God was there again, and Emanuel made his flight—barely. He was searched—the Nazis seemingly hoping to find any detail they might question him about—but nothing turned up that would serve their deadly mischief. Once out of Germany, Emanuel had a much easier time getting to Argentina.

Jews didn't have much choice of destination in those times, and Emanuel knew no Spanish, but putting thousands of miles between himself and the Third Reich was the idea, and Argentina served the purpose nicely. A large Jewish community had sprung up there as the Jews fled Europe, and the mission field would again be richly ready to harvest.

Breathing thanks to God, Lichtenstein set out for South America.

The customs officer's question remained in his mind as he traveled, and indeed he has never forgotten it. "Why does a Jew need a cross?" What a pointed question! How appropriate for a missionary to the Jews. Lichtenstein was spending his life answering that question, primarily for the benefit of Jews, not Nazis.

"I have ever since repeated it to myself every morning that He lets me see and every night as I lie down to rest, late as it may be," Lichtenstein writes in his memoirs. "In those few words," he goes on, "there is what the work amongst Israel—there is what the *entire* work of our mission stands for, and our whole task amongst the chosen people of God. In finding and conveying the correct answer to this question is all the success and all the failure of our mission and its work."

Unwittingly, that petty customs official gave Emanuel Lichtenstein great inspiration. God again used the wrath of men to praise Him.

The ABMJ installation in Buenos Aires thrived under the expert leadership of Lichtenstein, with whom the immigrant Jews could easily identify. The missionary had at least as dramatic an escape story as any of them, and he spoke their languages. He offered great comfort to those whose relatives had been left behind and the greatest of futures to those who believed the gospel. Mrs. Lichtenstein held an open house each week for quite a crowd, in addition to helping her husband with two services each week at the mission.

Lotte Furth turned up and served as a nurse at the mission dispensary, testifying constantly to her patients from her new Bible-school knowledge of spiritual things. The mission grew steadily, as the Jewish community of Argentina became the third largest in the world, after those of the United States and Israel.

Lichtenstein's memoirs from the decades of his Argentine mission work are replete with "the usual" front-line

Jewish evangelism stories ("the usual" in quotation marks because these stories are invariably so *un*usual, as missionary work goes). As the ministries of all the other personalities highlighted in this book, Emanuel Lichtenstein's work deserves a book of its own and can only be reported incompletely here. The best of his recollections follow. It is to be understood that they hardly reflect the joy and the tears, the year-in and year-out labor that Emanuel Lichtenstein gladly invested in his people.

In 1952 Emanuel received a letter from a rabbi who had received the help and consolation of the mission throughout his wife's grave illness. Mrs. Lichtenstein, as it happened, was also sick at the time, but not so seriously as the wife of the rabbi, who underwent her tenth operation in that year. The interesting part of the situation was that the rabbi was *not* one of those Jewish souls saved by the efforts of the mission. He instead represents one of the army of Jewish people constantly helped by the ABMJ through the years, "free of charge," so to speak. A Jewish person does not have to receive the Messiah to enjoy the attentions and the prayers of the mission.

The rabbi wrote:

VERY DEAR PASTOR:

When there is somebody so deep in distress as we are on account of my wife's illness, and when there is hardly any hope in the doctors' abilities nor for the restoration of health, what would give us more strength than the security to have good friends who sympathize fully with us and help whenever help is needed?

You yourself have belonged to these friends for a long time, even though our different occupations and sorrows do not allow us to meet but at long intervals. But whenever a threatening rock seems to stand in the midst of our way, we see your kind help drawing near us. More even than for the actual help we thank you for your indefatigable kindness and readiness to assist us.

May heaven reward you for it in the way that your dear wife be restored to health and yourself receive nothing but satisfaction and joy in your work.

Once more I ask you to accept my deep-felt thanks and our best wishes and blessings, as we have nothing else to offer you.

In friendship as ever. . . .

"Faithful to our missionary duties," writes Lichtenstein in humility, "we try to help every child of Israel that is in need, regardless of whether he or she has accepted the Lord or not."

Emanuel Lichtenstein was occasionally called to assist at a burial service. Such cases were usually concerned with cremation, at which no rabbi would officiate. The Jewish missionary was called forth despite the unsaved state of the deceased; an "apostate" prayer was better than no prayer, in the eyes of the family. In 1958 Lichtenstein assisted at such a burial, selecting his message from a Jewish hymnal and including the Jewish *kaddish* for the dead. He records that during his usual interview with the family in such circumstances, he received this time the commendations of a Jew who attended and had declared himself an "atheist incarnate." This atheist was touched by the very idea of Lichtenstein's willing help to the unbelievers around him. But the missionary was discouraged. He writes, "It is then (in death) that they think of the Jewish missionary, to whom before they have never found their way."

The story was given in Lichtenstein's memoirs under the heading "No Rabbi Will Assist."

The missionary to the Jews has to be ready for almost anything, working with a creative, sensitive people whose almost legendary depth of character and intellect must always be reckoned with. But the baptism of a certain twenty-one-year-old Jewish girl presented a brand new challenge to Emanuel. This girl knew nothing of Judaism and therefore had no background to appreciate that Jesus was the Messiah, or that anyone needed a Messiah for that matter.

He records, "Here was a case I had never experienced before. It is clear that the prophecies of the Old Testament will always be the center of our prebaptism instruction, indicating and showing our Jewish friends that Jesus is the true Messiah of Israel. But this otherwise intelligent and well-brought up girl knew nothing at all of the religion of her fathers, and the few stories she did know, she knew mostly wrong."

It was much more usual for Emanuel to gear up for discussions of great profundity in Scripture, Jewish custom, and tradition; in an odd way, the girl was a difficult challenge.

She was the only child of a lawyer, and the only hint of Judaism in her home was the forbidding of the mention of Jesus Christ. She had never held a Bible in her hands, had never worshiped at all—didn't know enough about God even to represent herself as an atheist. Lichtenstein laments the awful repression of religious studies in Vienna, where the girl had been raised, during the "social democratic regime." To the missionary, so cultivated in both Testaments, the girl's lack of comprehension of anything spiritual was grotesque.

But she still sought peace and reconciliation with God, Whom she felt truly did exist. She had come to the right place, though she certainly confused the expert missionary.

Emanuel Lichtenstein undertook to teach this unique prospect for salvation the whole of Judaism and the whole of Christianity. This faithful Jewish worker simply could not picture a Jewish person coming to Christ without first appreciating Judaism, and so he determined to completely fill the vacancy in her heart, preparing a complete Jewish Christian. He actually preached "private sermons" to her, always showing her the biblical text from which he drew his concepts. Probably few people besides Nicodemus had been given such a complete answer to a spiritual longing as that Jewish girl in Buenos Aires.

It took a long time. When Easter came around, Lichtenstein prepared a sermon on 1 Corinthians 5:7 ("Christ our passover") combined with Isaiah 53 ("a lamb to the slaughter"). He carefully compared the mission of Christ, the Lamb of God, to the Passover lamb sacrificed in Egypt. But he found that she did not know about the lamb in Egypt! It was slow going.

Lichtenstein writes a controversial statement, which he or any other truly knowledgeable Bible student could easily defend: "She was highly astonished to hear that knowing about Christianity was not possible without first studying the Jewish religion, because Jesus stems from the Jewish people according to the flesh."

People are saved every day, of course, without knowing about the Jewish religion or the Old Testament, but Lichtenstein would probably argue that they still did not *really know Christianity.* When this particular missionary brought an individual before the Lord, that individual was truly *ready* to meet the Lord.

There was a momentary hesitation about baptism on the part of Lichtenstein's protégée because she was not certain of her parents' opinion on this difficult point. Jewish people regard baptism as the point of no return, of course, and while Judaism wasn't really practiced in her family, the girl ran into some opposition. Eventually, however, the change in her personality was noticed, and her salvation given due credit. She was baptized by Lichtenstein, her parents not attending but tacitly approving.

Exactly the opposite challenge was presented to Emanuel in the person of respected Jewish leader Hirsch Beham, Zionist activist in Argentina and vigorous supporter of the Jewish state in Israel. Beham studied the New Testament on his own, having come into contact with many Christian people as a part of his tireless work for Israel and Jewish welfare in general. With a mind adept at understanding the Scriptures and a complete knowledge of the Old Testament, Beham came to the Lord on his own, solely from the truths of the Bible. He was baptized by a preacher in Argentina, with the warm approval of his wife, an active Christian.

But he came to Lichtenstein for more knowledge.

That was different, too. Not very many *Christians* walk into the mission saying, "Tell me about the Lord."

Lichtenstein provided his new pupil with a Yiddish New Testament, published by the ABMJ, and definitive lessons in the relationship of the two Testaments. Like a seminary student, Beham soaked up the intricate knowledge of prophecy, biblical types and symbols, and the history of ancient Israel. The seasoned missionary Lichtenstein was equal to the task.

Beham went to testify to his faith before Jews and Gentiles at every opportunity. Lichtenstein writes, "[He] spoke with ardour of the good fortune that was brought to him by his conversion; he also said that it was his daily prayer that the political state of Israel might become a spiritually true Israel with Jesus on His kingly throne in Zion."

Beham, saved when he was more than fifty years old, was an impressive witness in the Jewish community and a powerful spokesman for the coming Kingdom in Israel.

On Palm Sunday 1962, Emanuel Lichtenstein reached seventy years of age but showed no signs of slowing down in his tireless ministry to his people. In fact he had a special pleasure that very day—he baptized a young new believer who had first come into contact with the Messiah through a booklet written by Rabbi Isaac Lichtenstein, Emanuel's illustrious grandfather. The fearless old Jewish Christian's ministry was still going on, so far from its original source!

The memoirs of Emanuel Lichtenstein continue in much the same vein, with many unique stories of salvations and much of the same drama associated with missions to the Jews everywhere. God continued this ministry especially long, so that Lichtenstein was able to write, "My 77th birthday had just been over." But it was a melancholy ocasion this time: "I felt some sadness, for this time my beloved wife was not present—she died unexpectedly in 1966—but also great thankfulness, for I saw many a face among the attendance that I had not seen for some time."

The aged missionary now took the opportunity to bow out of formal mission service, passing the leadership of the Argentine Mission to his assistant, Pastor von Hefty. Von Hefty spoke English, Spanish, Hungarian, and German, and was a valuable help to Lichtenstein throughout his long tenure.

He left his work with joy, exclaiming that von Hefty was "a birthday present for me, for thus I can dedicate all my strength that is still left me to the Mission to the Jews, as long as God lets me do this work."

8

The American Connection

CLARA RUBIN

The testimony of ABMJ missionary Clara Rubin ties together nearly fifty years of American missionary history. She was practically born in the ABMJ headquarters on Throop Avenue in Brooklyn and still continues to labor in the New York area.

Many distinguished mission names already mentioned in connection with the foregoing testimonies come up in the story of Mrs. Rubin also. Her ministry goes on, after the decades.

In connection with other testimonies, the Jewish scene abroad during the difficult times of European persecution was described in some detail. But in the testimony of Clara Rubin, a clear picture of Judaism in America and the life of the early twentieth-century immigrants emerges. Mrs. Rubin particularly describes in fine detail the services at the Throop Avenue Mission.

One has to picture these particular immigrants, different from their Gentile counterparts in that every one of them had fled his homeland, rather than choosing to leave.

CLARA RUBIN (December 16, 1916–) founded the Huntington, Long Island, branch of the American Board of Missions to the Jews.

They came to this country with customs that the Europeans had become used to over the time, but that stood out in bold relief in Gentile America. Many of the married women wore wigs as a sign of subservience to their husbands; most of them spoke only Yiddish and their native European language. The men were talented and bright, by and large, but virtually shell-shocked from their experiences before immigration.

Eastern America was pioneer country for the immigrant Jews. They passed through the procedures at Ellis Island and into the Jewish communities, dumbfounded by all that they saw and heard in a totally new and different world.

The mission accommodated them as much as possible. The Friday and Sunday night meetings were always held in Yiddish, and Jewish hymns speaking of the Messiah were sung.

Mrs. Rubin tends to use the term *true* in front of the word *Christian* in her recollections of the distant past of the Brooklyn mission. The true Christians, she writes, were especially benevolent at Thanksgiving and Christmas:

> The week of Thanksgiving, true Christians from nearby churches would come and prepare an entire Thanksgiving dinner for all the mission families. An Episcopalian minister who loved the Jews would attend wearing the priestly collar, and many Jews seeing him would be afraid to come in, saying, "See—a golloch, a golloch," mistaking him for a Catholic priest, and saying, "This proves the mission is trying to make goyim of us."
>
> Christmas time at the mission lives forever in my heart. After the program, which we children took part in, shopping bags filled with candy, fruit, and gifts for each member of the family were distributed. Each year, Miss Sussdorf called out families according to size, to expedite

emptying the room. In the bags were Sunkist oranges, which, to us poor people, were something for the millionaires to eat.

For special outings at end of season and end of month-long Daily Vacation Bible School, we rode large, open-air, jitney buses to park or beach, singing all the way there and home. This, too, was a millionaire's treat.

I remember my kindergarten teacher at the mission, Miss Amy Blomquist, tall, very beautiful, and very loving. Her hair was in beautiful braids around her head or over her ears. Her smile was from ear to ear, and after our lesson with her, we would be served cocoa and broken cookies on our little kindergarten chairs. Our mothers would be in the next large room doing embroidery work and then, after their Bible lesson, would also enjoy cocoa and cookies.

Clara's mother first visited the mission, being treated at the dispensary, in 1915, a year or so before Clara was born. There was a big sign on the mission wall: "Every true Christian loves the Jews." This sign had a rather strange impact on the immigrants, because the majority of them had seen persecution in Europe in the name of Jesus—the horrible Good Friday massacres of Russia and the generally belligerent attitude of the nonbiblical Christian church toward the Jews remained seared into their memories. The sign was the cause of some discussion.

After Clara's mother was treated at the mission, missionary Augusta Sussdorf extended her an invitation to attend the meetings. Clara's earliest memory of accompanying her mother to the mission concerns the little child tearing up a Yiddish New Testament on the floor for her amusement during a meeting. She actually remembers the patient missionary Sussdorf praying, "God, You promised me Your Word woudn't return void."

It should be understood by this time that the attendance of a Jewish child at the mission was something of a disgrace in the community. The Orthodox Jews believed that the alchemists at the ABMJ changed Jews into Gentiles. Many false rumors were spread about the goings-on at the meetings, but Clara reports, "The mission showered us children with love and kindness—something we missed at home."

Clara had a shocked awakening when she started Hebrew school at ten years of age. There she learned the Old Testament stories and found that they agreed precisely with the stories she had learned at the mission. Until then, her concept of the mission and the synagogue was that they were opposites—now, she found they were teaching the same Bible. She writes, "So I knew the Mission taught me real Jewish things." She remembers crying during a mission film that told the story of Christ, and realizing that His unjust death did atone for her sins, as the mission taught. She received Christ at the age of fourteen.

The energetic teenager Clara Rubin was not an exemplary Christian. She writes, "I accepted Christ, but it was merely a head belief. I did as I well pleased. My behavior was atrocious, and I continued to be mischievous to Miss Dorothy Rose, my teacher, causing her more sorrows. As for Jesus, my attitude was—'Yes, it is true—but so what?' "

Clara continued to study the gospel in depth under the superb teaching of Rabbi Leopold Cohn, the mission founder. The lessons were always in Yiddish for the benefit of the constituency of the mission. Dr. Joseph Hoffman Cohn, Leopold's son, was also one of Clara's teachers.

Clara's mother had not received Christ, and when she saw that her daughter was serious about her studies in the gospel, she tried to stop her. No Jewish boy would want to marry Clara, the young girl was told, and she would be forever without a husband. Clara's parents put up with much embarrassment because of their daughter's tenacious attendance at the ABMJ.

As it happens, Clara's mother was wrong about no Jewish boy wanting to marry her Christian daughter. Joe Rubin, unsaved as he was then, came into Clara's life and presented her with an opportunity for a really practical witness.

Joe was an orphan, having been raised at the Daughters of Miriam Orphans' Home in Clifton, New Jersey. Joe was discouraged during those Depression years and hitchhiked coast-to-coast, ending up in Hollywood, California.

But God had anticipated him. The Reverend Elias Zimmerman, our dear friend "Zimmie," was already laboring in that field, and he taught Joe carefully and lovingly about his Messiah. But it remained for Clara to take the young man who was to become her husband to the ABMJ mission back on the East Coast in order to see his salvation.

In one of those remarkable situations of seed planting and later harvesting, Zimmie was to meet Joe some twenty years later and see the results of his teachings. They met at the funeral of Dr. Joseph Hoffman Cohn. Finally, ten years further along the road, Joe and Zimmie found themselves working together at the ABMJ's booth at the World's Fair.

Clara continued her work at the mission, teaching and witnessing among the children. The mission was a place for serious study. The children memorized whole chapters of the Bible and won prizes for doing so. Clara was still galvanized by the goodness of the mission's staff, as was her family to some degree. Clara's brother admitted that if

Miss Sussdorf were a Catholic, that church would have made her a saint. Clara supplies a story of Miss Sussdorf's ministry on an occasion when Clara was confined to the hospital:

> Miss Sussdorf was in her 80s, and a diabetic. I tried to keep from her that I was in the hospital and operated on. But she found out, took 3 buses, and came to visit me there. When I went home, she came in a pouring rain, saw I was in pain, said nothing, went home, and came again with her own heating pad. And she took 2 buses in the pouring rain to go home and come again. Who else but a saint would do this?

Children came to the mission as Joe and Clara continued to serve. In the summer of 1940, the mission opened a camp for children, and the young couple volunteered to help run the place. This was during the period when they were conducting a remarkable street ministry, giving the gospel on street corners while their eleven-year-old daughter played the accordion to attract the crowd. The Jewish people must have thought this incredible burlesque of spiritual matters was almost comic, but, again, the seed was sown.

Serious trouble struck soon after. Written in 1956, Clara Rubin's report of the situation is a kind of sermon in itself. Her English is good, and her faith most touching.

> I am not a professional writer, and my vocabulary is somewhat limited, but I write sincerely from the heart. Perhaps this letter will help to encourage others who may find trouble striking them unaware.
>
> Here we were, reaching the height of our ambitions. For the first time in our lives, we were now going to live in a decent place. We had worked so very, very hard for so many years to save money for a down payment on this

house. My husband was reared in an orphan home, and I was a child of poverty and slums.

We happily bought some new furniture and appliances, and our hearts were filled with a bursting happiness that our daughter would have a nice home.

Two weeks after moving, in escrow, trouble hit us like a bomb.

At 4:00 o'clock a.m., while driving to work, a car behind my husband, Joe, blinded him with the lights, then swung in front of him, cutting him off, and Joe struck an electric light pole. The other car sped away, leaving Joe helpless.

But for the grace of God, I was to have been with Joe. My parents had moved, the same week I did, to an apartment in the low-income city project. I had been going in to help them set up their place. The day before, my sister and my nephew came, and we decided to take the morning train, so as not to disturb my nephew. Instead, I got a call that Joe was in Flushing Hospital with both legs broken at the knees, the right one in three places, his jaw broken in three places, internal injuries, the muscles in his stomach and groin unable to function normally, etc.

After leaving Joe, I went to my parents. I spent the rest of that day trying to place my father, who was ill, into a hospital. I returned at 11:00 o'clock p.m. to my mother, that mission accomplished, too. I never saw my father again. Five days later, he was dead.

Most of my family and friends, including our daughter, were away enjoying their summer vacation. But God is *never* on vacation, and so I turned to Him. Let me show you, friends, how great is God's faithfulness to us, if we but take Him at His Word. He gave us the Bible, His Word, showing us how to come to Him. He gave to us the Holy Spirit, to dwell within us, to comfort us, and He gave us His promise never to leave us, and that He would supply all our needs according to His riches in Glory in Christ Jesus, and He gave us the wonderful privilege of talking to Him through prayer, with full assurance that He answers prayer. He promised us grace and strength sufficient for the day, and that He would carry our burdens, if we but let Him.

Three weeks later, Joe signed the papers enabling us to take title to the house. The doctor planned to set his jaw the next day. But that night, Joe had a major heart attack, and further work on his jaw had to be postponed, causing his jaw to set improperly. The doctors asked me to put private nurses on the job, as Joe's condition was very critical.

Again, I turned to God in prayer. I told God that nothing is impossible for Him to do, that He is the greatest Physician. The Bible says that Jesus is the same yesterday, today, and forever. Jesus healed the sick yesterday, and He can heal the sick today. I asked God that His Will be done, not mine, as He knows what is best for us.

I told God that we were His children, members of His chosen people, Israel, who were born again, of the Spirit and the Blood of Jesus, and that He surely cares for us.

I asked God to supply us with nurses, and He did. In the conference held just that week at the American Board of Missions to the Jews, many people prayed for Joe. In the audience were two nurses, both on vacation . . . one from Washington, D.C., and the other from a hospital in Brooklyn. Both these nurses volunteered for duty, and so faithfully and loyally watched over Joe more hours than a regular shift for nurses in a day.

Several nights later, Joe developed blood clots on the lungs. Again, doctors said his condition was critical, and he needed a miracle of healing. A volunteer nurse was instrumental in saving Joe's life. At night, the clot was dissolving, and, as Joe's mouth was wired shut, it was impossible for the blood to come out. Joe could have choked to death were it not for the nurse's watchful care.

I faced the hardest tests when I had to see Joe in such

dreadful pain. But, as I prayed, I realized how God could see His own Son, the Messiah of Israel, suffer the pain of death, and, because of this pain, the world received salvation. I would tell Joe, "God has plans for you, and good must come from your suffering. Perhaps God has work for you to do for Him, and this is the only way for Him to mold you to His Will," and with that, I would be comforted.

Again, we had another volunteer nurse from the Mission to replace the nurse who had to return to work. In the most critical times, God did not forsake us. Then, weeks later, Joe was operated on . . . his jaw had to be rebroken. Joe had two hemorrhages. A missionary friend of ours, Helen Koser, returned from her vacation the day before. She found in her house a letter from another missionary, Miss Sussdorf, telling her about Joe. The next day found her at the hospital in time to witness the operation. She put two nurses on duty for two days, again proving that God answers prayer, even without our knowledge, if we but trust Him. I knew nothing of this until it was over, as I was at home, 25 miles away from the hospital, getting my daughter ready for school. Another loyal missionary teacher, Miss Bullock, gave up her Labor Day weekend vacation to stay with Joe, that I might go home and rest.

I asked the Long Island paper, *Newsday*, to help me get a wheelchair for Joe. Through this notice, I not only got a wheelchair, from the American Legion in Huntington, but a minister, a stranger to us, called me and got me the loan of a hospital bed and paid for the ambulance to take Joe home from the hospital. This he did through the Melville Lions Club. The Red Cross in Huntington loaned me the mattress for the bed. Thus, Joe was able to be home for five weeks, with both legs in casts from thighs to toes, and his mouth wired up. We thank God for such helpful friends . . . vessels that were used by God to answer our prayers.

Now, we come to the part where we must continue to have our daily needs. I told God that He is rich, that He holds the wealth of the world in His Hands, and that I wouldn't ask or beg for money, etc., that He must and would supply our needs. I didn't ask a soul for money, yet money kept coming to us through the mail, from friends who heard about us through other friends . . . from people we had helped so many years ago, and forgotten about . . . from friends of Joe's who used to come into the store where he worked. Several times, these customers collected money and sent it to us. From the American Board of Missions to the Jews came help. And even from such very poor people, whom I had befriended, and who could very well have used the money themselves.

The hardest thing was accepting this money and help. The Lord had blessed us for the past 11 years to be on the giving end, and to have to receive was hard. But we thanked God for His faithfulness to us in supplying all our needs.

Even for Christmas, we received baskets of food from people nearby . . . and still, I didn't have to ask or make known our troubles to them. Someone else told them. God never forsakes His own.

We thank God for the doctors who watched over Joe day and night with such loving care. Never have I seen doctors display such kindness and interest. And the nurses and employees at Flushing Hospital . . . everyone hovered over him with such love . . . and everyone prayed for him there, too.

All along, I would tell the doctors there that Joe would pull through . . . because prayer all over the United States and Canada was going up for Joe, and God would not ignore the hundreds and hundreds of prayers going up daily. Doctors have the gift of knowledge, but God has the gift of healing . . . for which we praise and thank Him.

Now, almost six months later, Joe is walking again. Not

perfectly or very long, but we know with full assurance that God will restore him to health.

We know the day will come again when God will again honor us with the great joy of serving Him, and be able once again to help others who are in need. Once again, we will be back on the giving side and not on the receiving side.

We thank God for such a rich and full experience of His love for us. We rejoice that He chose us to know Him, and, because of Calvary, we will some day see Him face-to-face.

Should there be anyone who has trouble, let them turn to God . . . come to Him . . . His way as made clear in the Bible . . . then pray to God for help, and they will come through with much joy . . . the same as we have. If we could be instrumental in helping some person to do this, we ask God to use us for this purpose.

As if Clara and Joe Rubin didn't have trouble enough, they decided to start Bible classes for Jewish people in their home in Suffolk County in 1956. They sent out letters and issues of *The Shepherd of Israel*, published by the ABMJ, to over five hundred Jewish people every month. They borrowed chairs from the local undertaker and prepared to preach the gospel to the Jews.

At the first meeting, one of their daughter's classmates and her mother ran out of the place when they heard the name "Jesus."

A local rabbi called to tell Clara that because of people like her and Joe, Hitler killed the Jews. She quoted Scripture back to him, reminding him of Rabbi Gamaliel and Peter; she told him that if indeed the mission were not of God, the rabbi had nothing to worry about, but if it was of God, it shouldn't be touched. The Rubins had voluntarily taken on much persecution, and, although an entirely new generation of Jews was around them, they were completely ostracized by their Jewish neighbors, as in the old days.

Remarkably, after all of those years, Clara's mother continued her attendance at the Throop Street Mission. She had not come an inch closer to Jesus Christ in all that time, but somehow felt a peace at the mission meetings. But now, she seemed in her old age to join the persecutors.

Her new attitude was set off by an unfortunate happening when Clara and her mother were followed down the street by several angry Jewish women shouting abuse at them for attending the mission services. They also taunted Clara's mother by saying that Clara's daughter, Ilayna, now grown, would never be able to marry a Jew. Amazingly, the taunt of a generation before was renewed.

Clara writes:

> And in my mother's opinion, this was the worst fate that could befall a Jewish girl. And when Ilayna and I kept on attending the Mission, my mother stopped going. Both my mother and father said that if I continued to allow Ilayna to go to the Mission and get baptized, they would kill themselves.
>
> My heartfelt prayer to God, from the moment of her birth, when we dedicated our daughter to Him, was that God would give her, when the time came, a Hebrew Christian husband. This we felt would make it evident to all our Jewish friends that believing in Yeshua Hamashiach, the Lord Jesus Christ, didn't make us Gentiles, and that it would be a testimony to our faith in Him.

Ilayna was an attractive young lady and had several proposals from unsaved Jewish men, but invariably she would take her stand for Christ, and the proposals would evaporate. She was occasionally abused by those who professed to love her, when she made her spiritual feelings clear. Clara writes:

> My mother took this to heart and became critically ill. My family said I was killing my mother, and that my religion was a handicap to Ilayna. Why, they wanted to know, did we so desire that Ilayna marry a Hebrew Christian? I told them that we had dedicated her life to the Lord, and that God, in His own time, would provide a worthy husband for her. She was 21 years old, and her love for the Lord came first in her life, even before her love for her parents and her grandmother.
>
> I asked my mother, who was sick in the hospital, "How long do you want God to plead with you before you accept the Lord Jesus Christ as Messiah? You heard the Word of God 50 years ago at our Jewish Mission." She said she wanted a sign from God. I took her home and nursed her back to health. I prayed that the Lord would not let her die before she was saved. Shortly thereafter, God perfected that which pertained to me, as He had promised.
>
> On October 5, 1963, Ilayna was married to a Hebrew Christian young man whose parents are saved and are in Christian work. She is now Mrs. David Klayman. The marriage was performed by brother Daniel Fuchs, our Missionary Secretary, at a beautiful ceremony attended by many Hebrew Christians and others, and a whole host of unsaved relatives from as far away as Spain. They sat and listened to the message of the Gospel of the Lord Jesus Christ, Who was given preeminence on that occasion. David's father was brought to the Lord at a tent meeting in Brooklyn 29 years ago by one of the Mission's beloved workers, the late Joe Serafin.
>
> We found that it was also the 27th wedding anniversary of the Klaymans, and our own 26th! So the wedding

party became also a time of testimony to the sustaining
grace of our precious Lord.

My mother has now confessed that this was the sign
that she had asked God for when she lay ill in the hospital. She believes that Yeshua brought all this to pass because of our faith in Him. Once again we have the joy of
freely witnessing for our beloved Lord to all of our family,
and we pray that God will use us to His glory. How grateful we are to God for honoring our prayer that He would
provide a Hebrew Christian husband for Ilayna and to
use this family affair as a sign and a witness.

Again, as in the other testimonies, many of the dramatic
front-line stories have had to be omitted because of space.
But it is worth relating that a Yeshiva graduate met the
Messiah at the mission. The Yeshiva is the Jewish college
of rabbinical studies, and the graduates are steeped in the
Law, the commentaries, and the Scriptures. Mr. Martin
Fromm came forward to prove the mission wrong with
long years of study behind him and what he supposed to be
his incisive insight into the mind of God. He chose to confront the mission and the gospel once and for all. He ended
by utilizing his fine knowledge, plus the critical part of
God's mind, which he had previously lacked, as a mission
Bible study teacher.

Mrs. Rubin also reports the salvation of an entire family
of professed atheists, who now open their home for mission
Bible studies.

In addition, she was able, after sixteen years of prayer, to
speak in a large Jewish synagogue—the Beth El Temple.
The synagogue wished to have the evangelical event "Key
'73" explained so that they could understand it. Mrs. Rubin
instead held forth for two hours on the truths of the Gospel,
much in the spirit of Rabbi Isaac Lichtenstein, who

preached the gospel from the Orthodox pulpit in Hungary about the turn of the century. At this writing, Mrs. Rubin is still on the job, and her story of extraordinary salvations and many good works is simply typical of her mission.

If the ABMJ had to work without miracles, the labors of such as Mrs. Rubin would probably be not worth reporting. The results would appear too pale. But as things are and always have been with this remarkable outreach, miracles are just daily bread.

9

"To an Ancient People"

Leopold Cohn

In undertaking to write the testimony of the former rabbi Leopold Cohn, who became the founder of the American Board of Missions to the Jews, any author will be nearly overwhelmed by the timeless message of the original.
Rabbi Cohn wrote his own testimony under the title *To an
Ancient People* for the mission, which still distributes this
work. His magnificent life story, fresh and deeply moving
after the decades, continues to guide and inspire young
missionaries of today.

Rabbi Cohn was a profound, studious, disciplined, totally dedicated scholar of Scripture and lover of God.

This chapter will quote liberally from Rabbi Cohn's testimony. The following paragraph concluded his original
introduction:

> That this booklet may find its way over land and sea,
> from mountain to plain, into the hearts of children of God;
> breaking down barriers of prejudice, enlightening where
> there is ignorance, winning over where there is indiffer-
> ence, stirring up where there is lethargy, pacifying where

Leopold Cohn (1862-1937) founded the American Board of Missions to the Jews.

there is antagonism—for the spiritual welfare of poor, scattered Israel, and for the glory and honor of the Lord Jesus Christ, King of the Jews, is the earnest prayer of

Yours sincerely in His service,

LEOPOLD COHN.

July, 1908.
Brooklyn, N.Y.

The Reverend W. C. P. Rhoades also contributed an introduction to the original edition. His estimation of Rabbi Cohn's story should not be omitted here. "Doubtless, many will be interested in this simple, straightforward narrative. A life story surpasses all others. And in this life story the changes are so many and so great; the experiences are so varied and so deep; the motive so high and true, that sympathy cannot be withheld."

Rabbi Cohn begins his story simply.

I was born in 1862 at Berezna, a little town in the east of Hungary, where I was brought up in Orthodox Judaism. The Jews there look upon Christianity as a phase of heathenism, for the Catholics openly exhibit their idolatrous habits, prostrating themselves on the public highways before crosses and images, practices greatly abhorred by the Jews because they were forbidden to Israel by Moses. Their priests are generally addicted to drink and are bitter enemies of the Jews, inciting the peasants to injure them in every possible way. Because of these things, I was taught to avoid Gentiles, not even to take a drink of water from their vessels. The Jews know nothing of Jesus Christ and His claims to the Messiahship. They do not connect the two names, but think of Christ simply as referring to the word *cross*. They do not know of His teachings or of the existence of a book called the New Testament.

After seven years, Leopold Cohn was an orphan, his father and mother dying in the same year and leaving him to care for himself. He says, "Thus I early learned to trust God and often prayed Him to teach me His ways. When thirteen years old, I decided to study to be a rabbi or a leader of my people, the most honorable and meritorious life-office for a Jew."

The young scholar launched into the Talmud, a formidable study for a teenager. The Talmud comprises sixty books, which contain all the Jewish civil and canonical laws, and Leopold Cohn set out to learn the incredible intricacies of four thousand years of Jewish Scripture, custom, ceremony, and tradition. We can well appreciate his explanation of the law of the Sabbath.

> [This one commandment] is explained by the Talmudic doctors in four hundred and sixteen sections, each section containing from eight to twenty divisions, giving the most minute directions for the observance of the Talmudic Sabbath Laws. The Jews believe that all these, as well as the many thousands of rules and precepts appointed by the wise men, are as holy and binding as the ten commandments because they have a tradition that the Pentateuch, which Israel was commanded to put in writing, is only the text, and the Talmud is the explanation God gave to Moses by word of mouth on Mount Sinai.

At eighteen years of age, Cohn was proficient in Hebrew literature and Talmudic law, and he received from several rabbis in whose colleges he had studied, a diploma containing a certificate of his character and abilities. This gave him the authority to become a rabbi in his own right, and he was confirmed in that office by "my first and chief rabbi, a miracle-performer, S. L. Teitelbaum, in Sziget." He was immediately approached about an arranged marriage, and accepted his wife, Rose, according to the Jewish custom requiring that a sum of money be paid to the groom by the bride's father.

(This regional custom exactly reversed the tradition of the New Testament times, in which the bride's father received a sum of money from the prospective bridegroom for the privilege of marrying his daughter. The highest price a Jewish bridegroom ever paid for a prospective bride was that paid at Calvary.)

The eighteen-year-old rabbi's wisdom and skills became widely appreciated, and he was approached with questions and problems by Jews from near and far. He deferred often to his beloved master in Sziget, since it was not lawful for a disciple to rule on religious questions while his own teacher lived in the same district. But within a few years, upon the death of Rabbi Teitelbaum, his brilliant disciple was called upon to practice rabbinical duties in three congregations.

In truth, because of the community that he pastored, Rabbi Cohn was more of a lawyer and a judge than a spiritual leader. On every hand he decided difficult religious problems according to the lengthy learning he had undergone, and his flock abided by his rulings to the letter. He was often called to distant places to decide various cases.

Cohn continued his in-depth studies of the Talmud, reaching far beyond the normal requirement of study for the rabbinate. He became fascinated with the Talmudic doctrine.

> "The world is to stand six thousand years, viz., two thousand confusion and void, two thousand with the law, and two thousand the time of Messiah." Rashi, the very first and most authoritative commentator gives as an explanation of the last clause: "Because after the second two

thousand years, the Messiah must have come, and the wicked kingdom should have been destroyed." This greatly excited my attention. I was accustomed to sit on the ground almost every Thursday night at twelve o'clock, weeping, crying, and mourning for about an hour, over the destruction of Jerusalem (called by the Jews *Tickin Chazoss*) and repeating the 137th Psalm. I was very anxiously awaiting the coming of our Messiah, and now I saw that his time was over two thousand years ago, according to the Jewish reckoning. I was surprised, and asked myself, "Is it possible that the time which God had fixed for the appearance of our Messiah has passed away without the promise of our true and living God being fulfilled?" I never had had any doubt of the truthfulness of the Talmud; I believed every part of it to be holy, but now I looked upon this passage as a simple legend. It was then that I decided to search the Prophets concerning the time of the Messiah.

My first thought was to study Daniel, but I soon recollected that the Talmud curses one who studies concerning the end of the age, especially that part of Daniel which refers to the coming of the Messiah and the end of the times. "The bones of him who studies and calculates the ends" (meaning the time of the Messiah) "shall be blown up," says the Talmud. This sent terror into my heart and I thought that the minute I began to read that part of Daniel, a thunderbolt would come down from Heaven and strike me dead. But another thought came, suggesting that those Talmudists who made such statements must themselves have studied Daniel and the other Scriptures, concerning the coming of the Messiah, and if they did it, so would I. With fear and trembling, I opened the book, glanced over it, dwelling particularly on the ninth chapter. My research led me to blame myself for suspecting the holy words of the wise men. While I could see only as through a glass, for I was totally ignorant of Jesus the Messiah, who was cut off not for Himself, and therefore could not understand thoroughly that the Messiah must have died for our sins, yet I realized dimly that the Messiah must have come about four hundred years after Daniel was told by the angel about the seventy weeks (Daniel 9:24-27). There was gladness in my heart, to find it true that the Messiah should have come about that time, according to Daniel 9:24. But it was a joy mingled with sorrow. "Why has He not come?"

The modern reader must appreciate that Rabbi Cohn did not have access to a New Testament, nor did he even know of the existence of such a book. In his secluded, exclusively Orthodox Jewish community, the New Testament was utterly unknown. No one had so much as advanced a theory as to the discrepancy about the coming of the Messiah.

Concluding that the Old Testament must somehow contain the answer to the dilemma, Rabbi Cohn dug into it with resolve.

I, therefore, continued to study the Prophets with greater zeal. Whilst doing so, the pure spirit of God's Word took hold of my mind and heart. I then discovered that much of the Talmudic law is contrary to the Word of God. Then what a great struggle within, between light and darkness! I used to go into my large garden and, under an apple tree, cry like a little child, entreating, "Open thou mine eyes, that I may behold wondrous things out of thy law."

I could find no rest or peace for my troubled soul. I asked a good many other rabbis about the Messiah and how they reconciled certain passages of the Talmud with the Word of God, but I received no satisfactory answer. A little later, I was preaching, at that season, on a subject connected with the "Feast of Dedication" (Chanukah).

I had not intended to tell anything publicly of what was so deep in my heart, because of fear of persecution, but God, who causes the dumb to speak, opened my mouth, and I revealed unto them all my discoveries. Probably they would have believed the discovery about the Messiah, since we were all ignorant of the fact that such a disclosure related to the Crucified One, but when they heard me finding so much fault with the holy Talmud, that was quite enough to make them hiss and wag their heads at me, and finally to leave me quite alone, preaching to the empty benches. Bitter persecution followed.

The faithful parishoners of Rabbi Cohn must have been horrified to hear that honest sermon. But the rabbi's own regard for the truth overwhelmed any care about the reception his discoveries might meet.

So intent was this rabbi on the search for his Messiah that he began to travel to seek knowledge from rabbis in distant places. Few were amenable to discussing his questions in any way, and one finally offhandedly recommended America. "There you will meet plenty of people who will tell you more about the Messiah," said the rabbi, dismissing Cohn's queries. Singlemindedly, Rabbi Cohn immediately set sail for America. He did not so much as tell his family of his quest but left them behind, counting on a future reunion under the best of circumstances. He reached New York City in March 1892.

He was well received by a contingent of refugees from Hungary, some of whom knew him from the old country, and he was offered temporary service in a synagogue.

But of greater interest to Rabbi Cohn was his discovery of a peculiar church that bore a sign in Hebrew saying, "Meetings for Jews." Uncertain if he should enter a building displaying a cross on top, he hesitated by the door. A friend who knew him approached at that moment and advised him to quickly come away from there. They had a quiet interview in which his friend said, "There are some apostates in that church who mislead our Jewish brethren. They say that the Messiah has already come."

Rabbi Cohn had difficulty concealing his elation. Would there be someone at last who would at least have some idea of reconciling the Messiah's announced coming with the real Messiah? He walked away from the church with his friend until such time as he could excuse himself. He then sneaked back to the building and, taking a deep breath, walked in beneath the hated cross.

But Rabbi Cohn was shocked to see bare heads throughout the church and even the "rabbi" on the platform with his head uncovered. It was too much. He turned quickly and went out. But the janitor, noticing his confusion, provided the address of the preacher.

> The following Monday, I called on the minister and found him a Hebrew-Christian with a most interesting, winning way. He was educated in Talmudic literature, and when he told me that he was a descendant of a certain well-known rabbi, he gained my confidence and love at once. Seeing my utter ignorance of the Christian faith, but also my great earnestness, he gave me a Hebrew New Testament, asking me to read it. I opened it at once and read for the first time in my life: "This is a book of the generation of Yeshua, the Messiah, the son of David, the son of Abraham." My feelings could not be described! For many years my thoughts had been occupied almost continually with the coming of the Messiah. For that reason I had suffered and left my wife and children for a strange country, which I never expected to visit. I had inquired of several rabbis, searched the Scriptures, prayed and thought; my whole being was wrapped up in this one

subject. And now at last here was a book that would tell me about the Messiah. "Surely," I thought, "this book has come to me directly from above. God has sent it to me, and it will give all the desired information and lead me to the Messiah." The words "Yeshua, the Messiah, the Son of David," and "Son of Abraham" were sweeter to me than angelic music. I forgot all about my troubles and became very happy, and running as fast as I could to my private room, the doors of which I locked behind me, sat down to study that book. I began reading at eleven o'clock in the morning, and continued until one o'clock after midnight. I could not understand the contents of the whole book, but I could at least realize that the Messiah's name was Yeshua, that He was born in Bethlehem, that He had lived in Jerusalem and talked to my people, and that He came just about the time indicated by the angel's message to Daniel. My joy was unbounded.

It should be appreciated that a reading of the New Testament in Hebrew will not produce the name Jesus in any form. "Jesus" is a transliteration of *Ioesus,* found in the original Greek manuscripts of the New Testament. Rabbi Cohn was in the unique position of knowing well the character called Jesus (under His banner the Jewish people were so cruelly persecuted) and of knowing Yeshua, the Jewish Messiah, without realizing they were one and the same.

This brings up an irresistible point of discussion—that the average Jew had never seen the "Jesus" celebrated by the bloody hands of the Crusaders or the Inquisitors. Could he possibly connect Him, even in the vaguest way, with the loving Yeshua, Son of David, Son of Abraham? The cultivated Rabbi Cohn still had a lot to learn.

In his enthusiasm Rabbi Cohn approached his rabbi acquaintance to share his new knowledge.

In the morning, I ran quickly to my rabbi friend, who
by that time had already a prospect of securing a rabbinical charge for me, and told him of the book and my
discoveries. I had not identified this Yeshua, the Messiah,
with the name Jesus; I did not see at that time that this
Messiah is the same of whom gross caricatures had been
presented in my country, neither could I think of Gentiles
believing in the Jewish Messiah. Had that been the case,
humanly speaking, I could not have been reconciled to
that hated Crucified One. I thought that this Yeshua, the
Messiah, must be somewhere in this country, ruling as the
King, having His people, perhaps the lost ten tribes, as
His subjects, and what happiness it would be to join them
and to be under His rule! Such impossible dreams were
in my heart, and when I suggested them to the rabbi, one
can imagine what followed. Vehemently and with terrible curses, he threw the book to the floor, stamped upon
it, and in very unkind expressions, denounced me and said
that that was the book which the Crucified One had made,
and it was the cause of all Jewish troubles. "And now," he
said, "a Jew like you should not handle that book, or talk
or think of it."

Rabbi Cohn was astonished by the reaction of his friend
and the incredible news that the "Crucified One," the
"King of the Gentiles," was the subject of the New Testament.

I fled from his wrath with new struggles in my heart.
"Is it possible that Yeshua, the Messiah, the son of David,
is the very same person whom the Christians worship?
Why, that is idolatry! How can I have anything to do
with that?" For several days my heart ached with sorrow
and depression. Then I renewed my studies and began to
see the truth more plainly, as the sufferings of the Messiah
were revealed to me. The fifty-third chapter of Isaiah was

a most wonderful revelation, but what of it? How could I love that hated One? How could I take His name upon my lips since He is the Crucified One and since His followers in every generation and in every country have hated my people, robbed my brothers of all that was good and fair, killed, tortured, and degraded them? How could I, a true Jew, join myself to such a band of the enemies of my own flesh and blood? But a small voice seemed to whisper in my heart, "If He is the One of whom the Scriptures write, then you must love Him. No matter what others do in His name, you must do as He teaches."

Rabbi Cohn was of course in a terrible conflict, one faced eventually by us all. Should he accept what he clearly saw in the Scriptures and in doing so accept the hated Christ? Could he conceivably ever join the despised group he knew as Christians? The salvation of Rabbi Leopold Cohn is told briefly in a paragraph:

Halting between the two opinions, I decided to fast a day and pray God to show me what to do. At noon time, when instead of eating I began to pray, I held in my hands the Hebrew Old Testament and as I cried to God my body shook, and the book dropped to the floor and opened for itself. Opening my eyes, I looked down and to my great consternation, read from the open page, in the Hebrew, Malachi 3:1, which says literally: "I am sending my messenger and he shall prepare the way before me, and the Lord whom you seek shall suddenly come to His temple, even the angel of the covenant" (that word is identical with the word "testament") "whom ye delight in: behold, He has already come, says the Lord of Hosts!" I fairly began to shiver; like an electric shock the words went through my whole system, and I felt as if the Crucified One stood beside me, pointing to that verse and particularly to the expression, "Behold, He has already come."

I was awestricken and fell upon my face exclaiming with
all my heart, "My Lord, my Messiah, Yeshua, thou art the
One in whom Israel is to be glorified. Thou art surely the
One who has reconciled Thy people unto God. From this
day, I will serve Thee." At that moment, a flood of light
came into my mind and a stream of love to the Lord Jesus
into my heart, and straightway I went and took a meal,
breaking my fast and feeling altogether a new creature.

Coming to Christ brought Rabbi Cohn into a terrible
period of his life. He tried to speak of his faith and gladness to the Jews around him, but severe persecution resulted. The kindest theory advanced concerning the rabbi
was that he had lost his mind.

The bad news was sent to his wife in Europe and to his
former associate rabbi. All communications between Cohn
and his wife were stopped, as the community mourned him
as an apostate.

Rabbi Cohn was then forced to emigrate to Scotland.
The persecution from the American Jewish community was
more than he could bear, and a pastor from New York accompanied him to his new home, remaining to see him baptized in 1892 at the Barclay Church of Edinburgh. Rabbi
Cohn experienced terrible doubts—delusions caused by
Satan, as he described them—about his baptism, but he
managed to go through with this step of faith. This unique
baptism of a rabbi was greatly celebrated by the Christian
community of Edinburgh.

But the Jews there were angered. They wrote a letter
to a prominent rabbi in Europe, and they approached Leopold Cohn pleading with him to return to the Jewish faith.
But he demonstrated to them from the Scriptures: "To believe in Jesus was Jewish faith, real Jewish faith, and that

they had no Jewish religion whatever if they did not believe in the Son of God."

Struck by the scriptural evidence offered by Rabbi Cohn, the Jews proposed a kind of debate between Cohn and their own rabbi, and they hired a large private hall. The Jewish community came out in force to witness the argument. Rabbi Cohn humbly does not go into great detail about the debate but merely says, "The meeting lasted for two hours, the pride of the rabbi subsiding gradually with every answer to his questions until at last he had no more to ask. Then all went away, disappointed and discouraged, not being willing at the time to admit that this apostate was right in his belief in Jesus, the Messiah. Later on, some of them did acknowledge the truth as it is in Jesus."

In the midst of all of this spiritual triumph, Rabbi Cohn was deeply depressed by not hearing at all from his wife and children. He was unaware that his letters had not been delivered to her. Earnest prayers at Edinburgh for a reunion of his family finally caused Cohn to cable his wife, and communication was reestablished.

Mrs. Cohn wrote immediately to say that she had heard of her husband's alleged apostasy and simply asked what had caused those Jews in America to write such malicious and obviously untrue letters about her husband. He replied he wanted to see her very badly, ached for the company of her and the children, and would fully explain his position on the Messiah when they could meet in person. She sought the advice of a trusted rabbi and was advised to join her husband.

To do so was easier said than done. As she began to prepare for her trip, her relatives opposed her leaving.

> One of her wealthy uncles said that he would spend half of his fortune, if necessary, to keep her and the children

from me, for they too might be apostatized. He engaged a watchman, and prevented my wife's departure. This was a great disappointment, but my earnest friends were not discouraged and continued in fervent prayer to God.

I had corresponded previously with a number of my relatives who were much attached to me, explaining to them all about the Lord Jesus and His Messiahship. A nephew became especially interested and at last expressed his belief in Christ and continued corresponding with me in a very warm and affectionate way. Knowing I could trust him, I cabled him to arrange to take my wife and children by night and bring them to Berlin; and there another man sent by the friends from Edinburgh would bring them to Scotland.

Consequently, that nephew, an honest and experienced man, dealt wisely and assisted my wife and children after midnight when all was quiet and the watchman asleep. The Lord blessed his agency so that no harm befell them, and they reached Berlin in peace and safety. He notified me when they left town, and immediately a man was sent from Scotland to meet them.

In the morning when the watchman found what had happened, my wife's relatives tried to stop her by telegraphing to the train officials all along the route which they supposed she took, to detain thieves, but fortunately they went a different way and thus escaped the trap laid for them.

The first meeting between Rabbi Cohn and his wife was rather bitter.

I anticipated great joy upon meeting my wife after so long an absence, but was greatly disappointed, for no sooner did she see me than she said, "Tell me first about the rumor of apostasy!" It was then my duty to explain my position as briefly as possible, so I said the Crucified

One is our Messiah, and that all the time I was searching for the Messiah I did not know that it was He, but now I have found it out and would show it to her from the Bible as soon as we had opportunity. That was enough to confirm the report and she turned away, crying, and said that in a day or two she would return with her children, as she could not stay, on account of my belief in the Crucified One whom she had learned from earliest childhood to hate and abhor.

For two days and two nights, she maintained the same position, not looking into my face or talking to me. I felt very sad about it, for whenever I tried to explain my belief, she turned away and did not want to be in the same room; so I kept still, but continued in prayer to God.

Rabbi Cohn began with his oldest sons, nine and seven respectively, who knew their Bible well. He demonstrated the second Psalm to them, showing that God spoke there of His Son, and with childlike faith they accepted the teaching and joined their father in prayer. Unknown to them, they were overheard by their mother in the next room, actually praying for her salvation. Slowly the prayers were answered.

Two days later as I and the boys knelt in prayer, I suddenly felt her arm around me, and opening my eyes in surprise, I saw her smiling, though with tears in her eyes, while she said, "Do not worry, I will stay with you, for I see that you are the same child of God that you were. But I want you to promise to let me observe our religion as before. Then I will know that you are right." I agreed and we had a very happy hour; as the Lord showed His presence and gave us the peace that passeth understanding.

It was difficult to get Mrs. Cohn to read the Bible. According to Talmudic teaching, parents do not teach their daughters the Law. Thus, Jewish women as a rule are kept in ignorance of the Word of God. The sentiment that it is inappropriate for women to study the Scriptures dies hard, and Mrs. Cohn was loathe to look deeply into the new faith of her husband. She was a wife to him and even helped him in certain ways with his mission work among the Jews in Edinburgh and Glasgow where he held meetings. But she resisted coming to the Messiah in her own right.

Rabbi Cohn continued to testify, however, and particularly attempted to convince his wife through the first Passover Feast that they held together in Scotland. During the feast, the Jews take three loaves of unleavened bread, separated by linen, remove the middle loaf, break it and "bury" it beneath the pillow on the chair on which the father reclines. The broken loaf is recovered during the third cup of wine in the ceremony. Rabbi Cohn explained to his wife that the three loaves represent the Father, Son, and Holy Spirit. The middle loaf (the Son) is broken, "buried," and "resurrected" at the third cup, as the Lord Himself was broken for our sins, buried, and resurrected on the third day.

This beautiful demonstration of the gospel, done annually by Jews at every Passover table the world around, finally startled the rabbi's wife into searching the Scriptures and talking to the Jews about the Lord Jesus. Although she was not baptized until two years later, she could already see the truth, and she began to mention it in her letters to her brothers and sisters in Europe. The reaction was devastating.

> They became more bitter, and tried on one occasion to have the whole family extradited and brought back to Europe on some false charges. Mrs. Cohn's sister, who was very fond of her, enclosed in a letter a piece of black

ribbon and said that this would show that she mourns her as dead. This and many other annoying and harrassing letters enervated her very much and affected her health, although she had always been strong and well. On several occasions, when I had to meet groups of Jews for debates, she accompanied me and talked to them in a most remarkable way. She had much wisdom and a winning and convincing way of conversation. Once a number of prominent Jewesses in Edinburgh visited and besought her with tears to leave me and stay with them. They offered her an amount of money and wanted to assure her by writing that she would never lack friends or means, if only she would stay among the Jews and give up her apostate husband. But she refused, and told them that she knew her husband better than they did, and that she had more confidence in her husband than in all the Jews of Edinburgh. She also told them that they too ought to accept the Lord Jesus Christ.

The Cohns soon moved back to New York. Rabbi Cohn felt led to return to where his persecution had really begun and to become a missionary to the Jews there. The Cohns were nearly penniless when they decided on the newly-founded Jewish community in a suburb of Brooklyn called Brownsville.

Rabbi Cohn rented a store and on the following Saturday held his first meeting there. Eight Jews attended, and there was nearly a fight when the rabbi mentioned the name of Jesus. But the following Saturday sixteen Jewish men, hard eyed and skeptical, occupied the little storefront. It was lonely, difficult work.

There was not a single Christian to help me in that pioneer work, financially or otherwise. During week days, I had the mission open daily for a reading room, while in the evenings, I taught the Jews English by reading the

New Testament in English with them. Thus I tried hard
to make rapid progress by crowding a great deal into the
short days which seemed to fly swiftly away, carrying with
them so many Jewish souls without hope of salvation.

As the mission attendance steadily grew, leading Jews of
Brownsville became bitter, and several attempts were
made to do bodily harm to the new missionary. On one
occasion he was decoyed by a request to bring a Hebrew
New Testament to a certain house. There he was beaten
bloody, so that he could barely drag himself home.

His wife, however, was still completely supportive of
the mission work and even offered her jewelry in pawn to
pay the mission rent. Money was so scarce that the family
could not eat properly, and sometimes the children only
had a cup of tea for their lunch.

But little by little Christian friends began to notice the
new work, and support drifted in to ease the burdens of the
Cohns. A particularly enthusiastic supporter was the Reverend T. J. Whitaker, pastor of the Bushwich Avenue Baptist Church, who raised the monthly mission rent in his own
congregation. He confided to Cohn that he, as well as
many other pastors, had never thought before of doing
mission work among the Jews. He faithfully attended
every meeting, sang for the little congregation, and helped
the cause in every way he could.

And little by little the mission began to prosper from the
efforts of its own converts. While the Gentile Christians in
many churches said, as they still say today, "There's no use
working among the Jews—they cannot be converted," or,
"It's purely a waste of time," the mission went on bringing
the Jews to Christ. Rabbi Cohn writes of many dramatic
conversions among his people, particularly that of one
outspoken Jewish anarchist, who used to come to the meet-

ings cursing, grinding his teeth, and shaking his fist in Cohn's face.

Before long, that man had to confess before the other Jews that there is no truth but in Jesus. There were several cases where two or three in a family were converted and some whole families. There was the case of a Jewish lawyer who was converted, his wife and his six children with him. He used to keep an open Bible on his desk, and when his clients came in, instead of talking business with them as usual, he called their attention to what he had found in the 53rd chapter of Isaiah and other passages, showing that Jesus is the Messiah. He was bitterly persecuted as a result of his confession and had to leave Brownsville, for on one occasion, they attempted to set fire to his house.

Christian ministers as well as laymen began to rub their eyes and ask themselves, "What does it all mean?" Many Jews used to come to my house privately during the week to inquire more fully about the truth, for when they attended the meeting they could only listen. My dear wife used to take a great deal of pains explaining to these Jews, and told them of her own history. Nearly all those to whom she talked went away with strong faith in the living God and in His word about the Messiah. She soon gained the confidence of the Jewish men and women, who had great respect for her tact, wisdom and godliness, as she grew stronger and stronger in the faith. Still, Satan put many temptations in her way to repel her from Christ. For instance, our children who went to Sunday School, used to be persecuted by Christian children who called them names and sometimes tried to do them bodily harm. The children used to come home crying and tell their mama how the others called them names, but she, with true motherly love, took them in her lap and comforted them, telling how the Lord Jesus suffered and how Elisha, the great prophet, was called names by a lot of children. Thus, with great sorrow in her heart for the wounded feelings of her children, she knew how to comfort them and still remain steadfast in the Lord Jesus Christ from whom such things could not separate her.

On one occasion a number of boys took one of my boys, who was only six or seven years at that time; they stretched him on the floor, some holding him down while another stepped on his legs below his knees and fractured them. In spite of the agonizing screams of the boy, they laughed and said, "That is the way the sheenies cry." Then the boy was brought home helpless and one can imagine what great grief and vexation that caused us, and I thought, "Now her faith will be weakened," for Jewish people used to come in and when they learned of it, say, "You see with whom you have to associate and who Christians are." But the warm heart of my dear wife never gave way, but always kept on saying: "And so they did to the prophets who had to suffer to glorify the name of Jehovah, and so must we." Our little boy was sick for a long time in the hospital, but the Lord healed him and our joy was made full. On a later occasion, however, some other so-called Christian children took one of our boys, and while several held him by force, another came with a knife and cut his lower lip through and through, and said: "This is the way we have to do with sheenies." Many other trials came in different ways from the hands of so-called Christians, and I always felt worried lest they should repel either my dear wife or some of my children from the Lord Jesus Christ, but thanks be to God it was not so. All remained steadfast, heeding not such trials and persecutions, and after a short time, Mrs. Cohn was baptized by the Rev. W. C. P. Rhoades, D.D., pastor of the Marcy Avenue Baptist Church.

Financial difficulties continued to plague the mission for

some two years, until one Saturday about a dozen ministers and laymen of two Baptist societies attended a meeting. They offered their support to Leopold Cohn, who thankfully accepted with the stipulation that there should be no interference with his methods of dealing spiritually with the Jewish people. The Baptists continued their strong support for the next eleven years.

When the mission in Brownsville was thus running successfully on its own, Rabbi Cohn prayed about beginning a mission in Williamsburg, an old Jewish settlement in the city where there were then about fifty thousand Jews. He virtually started over again from "scratch," putting together gifts that totaled some fifty dollars for the first month's expenses. Rabbi Cohn had to call upon all his ingenuity in bigger, tougher Williamsburg.

> As the crowds that came to the meetings grew larger and their interest in the Gospel became stronger, the Jewish leaders waxed bitter. They tried hard to stop the flow of men to the Mission, but could not prevail against the strong tide, driven by the Holy Spirit. Jews began to become convinced that Jesus is really the true Messiah. Some of them confessed Him publicly among other Jews and were greatly persecuted. Now and then zealots came to the meetings and in the midst of the sermon, would rise and cry out, "Fire!" and in this way succeeded in getting a large number out of the hall. Once, these instigators gathered a crowd and came to the Mission, and at a given notice from their leader, began to upset chairs on which they sat, causing much confusion, and actually drove the people out of the meeting. They did this several times till I had to have a policeman, but even then they succeeded once in crowding him in the crush so that he was forced out in the crowd like a bullet from a gun. He fell down, lost his club and his hat. He was an Irishman and was

greatly surprised that Jews could beat him so badly. However, the Lord gave me much patience to ignore these excitements, and I continued giving my testimony for Him, having had divine assurance that no evil shall befall those who trust in Him and co-labor with Him.

Thus, a very busy time ensued. No help could be secured in a way of personal assistance in two active fields, as interest in the evangelization of Jews was almost non-existent among the dear Christian people. Just a few months before I opened the Williamsburg Mission, the Lord put it into my heart to gather children in the Brownsville Mission and work among them. I did not want to take them from the streets without their parents' knowledge as that would do much harm to the cause; so I went to those parents who attended the Mission and were somewhat interested in the Gospel and succeeded in getting thirteen girls to form a Sewing School. Now, sewing was a branch of education which I had never pursued, but I thought through Christ and for Him I could do anything; so I tried to teach the girls sewing. I met a Christian woman and asked if she would not come to help us teach in the Sewing School, but she said she could not go to Jewish children as the Jews are prejudiced and would not learn from a Christian or come to a mission. I told her that I had had one session and the children did come. "How many did you have?" she queried. "Thirteen for the first meeting," replied I. "Well," said she, "I would not come anyhow, because thirteen is a bad number to begin with." But soon the Lord raised up a few Christ-like women who came steadily and taught the girls sewing and the Gospel, especially two ladies who have been helping ever since that time and have not wearied in well-doing. The Lord is their reward. The number of children began to increase from the beginning until there were as many as two hundred, so that often we could not find room or teachers for them. Christian work among the

Jewish children is a very delicate matter. The children may see the truth in time, but as long as they are with their unconverted parents, they dare not confess Him or speak about Him at home, as they highly respect them. The idea of their parents' supremacy is inborn. So even if we did not hear of many conversions, their attendance at the meetings at least disarmed their prejudice and gave the girls a chance to learn about the Lord Jesus Christ. In this way, work among the children was greatly blessed. There soon were scores of mothers that as girls attended our Sewing School in the first two or three years, and they talked to their husbands about Christ. Once, standing in a street-car, hanging by a strap, I was surprised and embarrassed when a young woman, well dressed, rose and offered me her seat, calling me by name. I did not know her, but she was one of our Sewing School girls and remembered me very well and introduced me to her husband, saying: "This is the Rev. Mr. Cohn of whom I learned all that I told you."

The Williamsburg mission prospered under the ingenious leadership of "the Reverend Mr. Cohn." Many Jews were led to Christ and experienced the life-changing miracles of the walk with Him. Rabbi Cohn was especially grateful that so many went out to preach the gospel in their own towns. *The Chosen People,* the official organ of the mission, was established by Rabbi Leopold Cohn and is still issued monthly from the headquarters of what is now known as the American Board of Missions to the Jews.

Mrs. Cohn, increasingly ill through her final years, passed away in 1908. In her last feverish hours she confided to her husband an amazing vision.

"My thoughts are continually wandering away from me, up and up, far yonder they break through that mysterious wall and show me how I will meet Jesus there. My mind

pictures Him as sitting on a great white throne, holding
out a golden scepter as Ahasuerus did to Esther the
Queen." These words, as well as a number of other utter-
ances from her feverish lips during her last hours, revealed
her absolute faith in the love, mercy, and truth of the
Lord Jesus, who promised to receive His followers into
the prepared place; she never doubted, but could see her
way clear and straight to the presence of the King of kings
without any fear whatever. Such words could not but
confirm my conviction that there has not been a more
devoted Christian woman on earth. She was anxiously
waiting to see the much needed building for the mission
realized. She used to join me in a private prayer to God to
move upon the hearts of those dear Christians who have
the means and cause them to put up the building. She was
so sanguine and confident that she never doubted its realization. However, toward the end of her life when very
feeble, she said to me: "I have been pulling with you hard
up-hill for so many years, waiting for the Mission building and now, when almost to the top, the Lord wants me
to go away. I have asked God to let me live to see the
building and a Jewish-Christian congregation worshipping
the Lord in it, but He says no, just as to Moses when he
wanted to enter the Promised Land."

Rabbi Cohn concludes his autobiography with a tribute
to his wife and an expression of hope for Israel:

> For me, who am now left alone to complete the work
> for which we both sowed in tears, she will ever live, a con-
> stant inspiration and motive power in the carrying on of
> the work which was the supreme love of her life; until I,
> too, shall reach the yonder shore, and amidst the glad
> meeting and greeting, we both hear the "Well done, thou
> good and faithful servant."
>
> In loving appreciation and gratitude to God for such a

life and such an inspiration, I have written these pages, in the hope that the Lord will use them to the blessing and encouragement of many souls, and to the awakening of an unprecedented interest in Israel. Amen.

An addendum, added much later on, traces the continuing history of Leopold Cohn's work. The mission that began in a rented store in the Brownsville section of Brooklyn, and later became the Williamsburg Mission to the Jews, is now, as the American Board of Missions to the Jews, the largest Jewish mission in the world.

Rabbi Leopold Cohn died in 1937, and the management and responsibility of the mission passed to his son, Dr. Joseph Hoffman Cohn, who had labored at the side of his father many years previously. Dr. Cohn furthered the work until his own death in 1953 when the present leadership of Dr. Daniel Fuchs was instituted.

A current list of Zola Levitt's books, cassettes, albums, and videotapes is available at no charge from:

ZOLA
P.O. Box 12268
Dallas, Texas 75225